WAR STORY WEDNESDAYS:

CALIFORNIA REAL ESTATE LAW VOLUME 1

WAR STORY WEDNESDAYS

CALIFORNIA REAL ESTATE LAW VOLUME 1

A TRIAL LAWYER'S

TALES FROM THE TRENCHES

CHRISTOPHER HANSON, ESQ.

First Printing 2015

ISBN: 978-0986161315

This work was designed, produced, and published in the United States of America by

CARTWRIGHT
PUBLISHING
Visibility ▪ Authority ▪ Legacy ▪ Clients

145 Corte Madera Town Center, #415
Corte Madera, CA 94924
www.CartwrightPublishing.com
415-354-2388

Cartwright Publishing is always interested in publishing new non-fiction manuscripts from professional services providers such as attorneys, architects, CPAs, doctors, financial planners, inventors, and real estate professionals.

Register This Book to Get Free Updates and Free Videos

The topics covered in this book are also reviewed in a (mostly) monthly electronic newsletter we publish. If you'd like to be on that list, or if you have a "war story" for me, or if you'd like to talk to me about a specific situation, reach out to me through any of the methods below. (And, no, we don't sell the list or make it available to anyone else. Period.) When you sign up, I will also give you access to selected video presentations of these and other *War Stories*, and, occasionally, a presentation we've done at some conference or other. To get updates to this book, to get the newsletter, or to reach me and tell me your personal *War Story*, visit:

- www.WarStoryWednesdays.com or
- text: WSW to 58885 or
- phone: (415) 942-8291

Table of Contents

Introduction

Humans, it turns out, are lousy students. Our brains struggle with Western learning techniques. We, in every society around the globe, prefer the campfire of our caveman ancestors and learning by being told stories—just ask any five-year-old if she prefers school or a bedtime story.

Real estate brokers and agents, their clients, and sometimes even their lawyers are no different.

Ask most of those same people (the brokers, agents, and clients—not the five-year-old) if they have any interest in being told about a case from the California Court of Appeal, and they run, screaming for the hills. Case law, it seems, is no bedtime story.

I disagree.

We learn from stories. On my website, and in our eZine (a fancy name for electronic magazine / newsletter) I tell these kinds of stories, generally on the third Wednesday of each month. This book is a collection of more stories, all of which are based on cases decided by the California courts, designed to teach us what to do and what not to do.

Each of the cases described in this book is based on a true story. The cases involved real people who lost or gained real value as a result of a trial. Going through a trial, and then an appeal, is a serious thing. The emotional and financial tolls it takes on the participants can only be imagined by someone who hasn't lived through it. For the participants, it is a nightmare turned real. For one side or the other, it is ... a horror story.

But—stuffy case briefs are for the law library.

These stories are for the shelf next to your desk. I've—well— taken some liberties. I've embellished. I've made these "entertaining." Did I change any material fact? *Nope.* (At least, I don't think so ...) Did I give the cases flavor? *You betcha.* After all, I have to keep your attention, don't I?

Read. Enjoy. The errors are ALL mine and mine alone.

Christopher Hanson, Esq.
San Francisco, CA
February 2015

PS: I'm a lawyer, so the California State Bar has "rules" I have to follow. Many of those rules restrict how I can interact with "the public." So: This is NOT a solicitation for your business. If, after reading this, you think, "Oh, I've got to hire that guy," that's terrific. We'll talk. And I still might say, "No thanks." Another thing—this is NOT a legal treatise. This is NOT legal advice. This is me, waxing poetic. If you want real legal advice, contact a lawyer, create an attorney-client relationship by way of a written retainer agreement, write a whopping large retainer check, and hire yourself a lawyer. You know how it goes. All that said, read on.

1 |Agency

Before I begin with the first story, let me set the stage.

Have you ever wondered who actually gets hired when you walk in to a real estate brokerage and meet the nice lady at the front desk? Or into that open house down the street and decide that that's the person you want to work with to help you buy or sell a house? Or when you see a sign on the empty shopping center space that would be perfect for your dog-grooming business's second location?

I'll give you a hint: it isn't the nice lady. Ninety-nine percent of the time that person you meet isn't from a single person office. Ninety-nine percent of the time, the person you meet works for a person or a company that is THE broker, the person that the California Bureau of Real Estate (CalBRE) says is responsible to it for all the licensed activity undertaken by the *brokerage.*

There are two levels of licensure in California: a salesman's license and a broker's license. A broker can supervise salesmen. A broker can work independently, but a salesman must work under, or through, a broker. Oftentimes, someone who is a licensed broker will work for a different broker. That happens all the time.

A company can be a "broker" too. Many times, some poor soul works as the "designated broker" for the corporate brokerage and has all these other brokers and salesmen reporting to her. Many times, the designated broker is NOT the owner of the corporation. But she can do all the same deals. She can represent clients. When something goes wrong however, it's the designated broker that gets the call from the CalBRE or the plaintiff's lawyers.

Then we've got the agents (like the nice lady at the front desk) at the real estate offices who are working for the sellers, and different nice ladies at another office working for the buyers. One might be a broker, the other a salesman, and both working for the corporate brokerage.

So, with all these layers of everybody doing everything, how do you know who works for whom? Funny you should ask. So did a lot of other people. So many, in fact, that the California Legislature thought it would be a good idea to make sure all these agents and brokers made sure you knew who was working for whom, right up front.

There is a form (you'll hear a lot about forms in this book) that is required—in both residential AND commercial transactions—where the agent/broker/brokerage relationship is described and another where it is confirmed. Right from the very beginning, everybody is supposed to know who is representing whom and what the representative is supposed to do. Sometimes it even works out the way it's supposed to.

Here's why all this is really, really, important.

No matter if the person doing the work is a salesperson or a broker, the person or entity responsible for the end result of the work is the individual broker-owner or the company.

In this book, I refer to the person working for the brokerage as an "agent." It doesn't matter if that person is a salesman or a broker licensee. When I refer to the "broker" or the "brokerage," I usually mean the person that the "agent" works for, be it an individual person or a corporate entity. I say "usually" because I've been a licensed broker for 35 years or so, and I slip up now and then. I think of the agent and broker as a single entity and automatically think "broker" or "brokerage" when it is something an "agent" has done. After all, the broker/brokerage is ultimately responsible anyway.

To make matters even more confusing, I will refer to the relationship between the customer and the brokerage as an "agency relationship," even though it is not limited to the interactions between just the agent and the customer and has everything to do with the legal responsibilities of the brokerage to the brokerage's customer.

So here you are, an agent or a brokerage, both of you wanting to do some business. Or there you are, the landlord/tenant or the buyer/seller, looking for someone to help you out.

How do you form that representation with or as a customer? And, just what, exactly, are you responsible for in that representation?

In the first couple of *War Stories* I talk about just that.

You might be surprised to learn that you can form an agency relationship without a written agreement. Mind you I said, "Form a relationship." That means the brokerage just became responsible for its actions with regard to the representation of a customer's interests. It doesn't mean that the brokerage also earned the right to be paid for that work. To get paid, or rather to be able to force a customer to pay you if they decide not to, you have to have a written agreement

So let's start. Let's take a look at an example or two of the agency relationship itself.

The Case of the Veteran Investor

(Adapted from: Carleton v. Tortosa, 14 Cal.App.4th 745)

Let's start with a taxing situation—a 1031 exchange. For those of you unfamiliar with the Internal Revenue Code, a section 1031 tax deferred exchange allows a seller to sell one property, buy a second property of the same kind, and defer the payment of the taxes due on that sale until the second property is later sold. Of course, there is a lot more to it, but in a nutshell, that about covers it.

Here's a scenario where a sophisticated real estate investor, somebody who had been flipping homes for 25 years, hired a real estate agent to assist in the sale of two apartment buildings and the subsequent purchase of two others with the profits of those sales. The client did not structure the transactions as a 1031 exchange and as a result, ended up paying $34,000 in taxes. The investor could have deferred (and maybe even avoided) payment of those taxes if the sales and repurchases had been structured as a 1031 exchange.

Now, we all know that sophisticated real estate investors don't make mistakes. So it had to be somebody else's fault, right? As you might have guessed, the real estate investor sued the real estate broker for failing to advise the investor that a 1031 exchange was possible under the circumstances.

There was the obligatory trial and the almost inevitable appeal.

The Court of Appeal looked at the investor, listened to his sad story about why it was the brokerage's responsibility to warn him about the tax consequences of selling his buildings and to advise him how to save on or defer payment of taxes, and decided, "Yeah, not so much"—for a couple of different reasons.

First, the listing agreement itself said that if the customer wanted to get tax advice, s/he/it should go talk to a tax consultant. There was also, the court pointed out, a disclosure that was given to the investor that included specific language that referred to a portion of the California Civil Code that also says that if a client wants advice with respect to taxes, they are to consult an appropriate tax professional.

So, as a matter of law, the court concluded that the real estate broker had no duty to give tax advice or assist the client in structuring the transactions as a tax-deferred exchange.

That would have taken care of the case, as a one-off, but the court went beyond just the case in front of it and did something that is really helpful for a real estate brokerage.

The court held that the relationship between a client and the broker is defined by the scope of the retaining document, in this case, by the Listing Agreement, or in another, by the Buyer Representation Agreement. As a result, the court noted, the real estate brokerage can limit the amount of exposure it takes on when it's representing a client by limiting what the duties are inside that listing agreement or that representation agreement.

The trade associations in California representing agents and brokers have forms for listing agreements (and almost any other kind of general document used in a real estate transaction) that use as much language as can be mustered to limit the scope of the duties a real estate brokerage will owe a customer.

You may want to think about that if you're about to do a deal. From the brokerage's perspective, it can limit the potential liability a brokerage would owe a client. As a consumer of the professional services of a brokerage, a customer may want to broaden the scope of those very same duties. It is a sword that cuts both ways.

OK, we've now seen how a carefully crafted representation agreement may be all well and good for getting out of trouble. In the 1031 case, the representation agreement specifically said that there was no obligation to give tax advice. Whew. But what if there is no agreement? How would a broker or a customer know what the brokerage is responsible to a customer for if something goes wrong?

Who Pays When "It" Hits the Fan?

(Adapted from: Hicks v. Wilson, 197 Cal. 269)

Let's go back in time to 1925.

Some things don't change, like the fact that people want to buy property in Palo Alto and that they have real estate brokers from San Francisco who are there to "help" them. That's what happened here.

The customer and the broker talked about looking for a home in Palo Alto. One afternoon, they jumped in the Model T and headed on down the Peninsula. Low and behold, they found "just the right place."

The broker knew the seller, which made life convenient for everyone and pretty informal. So, as they were sitting in the living room talking about doing the deal, the customer asked the seller, "How much do you want for it?"

Before the seller could respond, the real estate broker jumped up and called out, "$6,125!" (If only that were the case today, right?)

The seller, sitting right there, in the living room of the house, nodded at the buyer and agreed, "Okay, I'll do that deal."

The buyer, looking back at the seller, asked, "So, how do you want to do this?" The seller, looking at the buyer, stated, "Talk to the broker. Deal with him." And off they went.

Back in San Francisco, the broker and buyer put together the purchase agreement, and the buyer wrote the real estate broker a check for a $3,000 deposit, arranged a loan for the other $3,125, and prepared to close.

That's when the broker took off with the money.

Everyone was now ... unhappy. The buyer would like either to get the money back or close the deal; and the seller didn't want to close the deal unless he was going to get the full $6,125. So they had a problem.

The buyer sued the seller for the return of the $3,000 he had given the broker.

The seller argued, "Well, wait a minute. He was *your* broker. He is your problem. He wasn't my broker—not at the time that you came to the house and made the deal."

It turns out that there was no listing agreement and that the real estate broker, on that first day when everyone was chatting it up in the living room, didn't have any contractual agreement with the seller of the property at all. The day *after* the buyer and the seller met at the property, the seller entered into a commission payment agreement with the broker—but that was after, not before, the deal was struck with the buyer. So there hadn't been a pre-existing relationship between the seller and the broker.

Once again, there was a trial; and once again, an appeal.

The Court of Appeal struggled just a little bit, saying, "Well, it's true that the buyer met with the broker in the first instance, but that's generally what happens; and it's true that the broker went down to the seller and said, 'I've got somebody that wants to buy your house,' but that's also, generally, what happens; and it's true that there was no official written agency agreement between either one of them."

So who's responsible for the loss?

The Court of Appeal found, "The triggering moment in this transaction was when the seller was sitting in the living room and looked to the buyer and in response to the question from the buyer —'Who do we deal with?'—pointed to the broker and said, 'Do business with him.'"

"At that moment," the court decided, "the seller made the real estate broker the seller's representative; and when the buyer handed the money over to the broker, that was the same as handing the money over to the seller."

Thus, the seller was found responsible for returning that $3,000.

The liability arose from what we call "ostensible agency." It's when you allow a third person to believe that this guy over here is authorized to act on your behalf, whether there's a written agreement or not; and if that third person, relying on that representation, does something with the person you said is your agent, then you are responsible for what your agent does, even if it's taking the other guy's money.

This, by the way, is the kind of thing that gives the owners of a brokerage night sweats. I mean, really, how can you control the actions of anywhere between 3 and 3,000 agents working for a brokerage? There are a number of bad apples out there. Not everyone, certainly. In fact, I'd say that the vast majority of real estate agents are honest, hard-working people, who really do want to do the best job they can for their customers.

But, let's face it, the regulatory requirements to get a real estate license are not terribly difficult. And once licensed, an agent/broker has access to tens of thousands, or hundreds of thousands, of their customers' dollars. The temptation can be overwhelming, especially when it's been a long time between commissions.

Which leads to the next story of our *War Story Wednesdays* ... deciding who the client is.

How Old for Mold?

(Adapted from: Coldwell Banker v. Salazar,
117 Cal.App4th 158)

Here we had a couple that scrimped and saved and scrimped and saved and finally bought their first house. They had kids— three little ones. Only about 6 months after moving into the "home of their dreams," the kids started sniffling and sneezing and hacking. That just wasn't good. A little bit after that, one of the kids started to have really labored breathing. And a little bit after that, they took the kid to the doctor and discovered he had developed asthma.

They began looking around trying to figure out what in the world was going on to cause the illnesses everyone was suffering from. They looked around the neighborhood, the house, the pets, and anything else they could think of. Finding little, they went back to the house and looked some more, and they found a water leak and discovered mold growing all throughout the house.

And not the mold like you find on an orange but that nasty, black *stachybotrys*—toxic, ugly, "hurt you bad" mold.

These folks were not happy, not even a little bit. They sued the sellers and the real estate brokers and everybody else that was supposed to have discovered this mold because, it turns out, the leak had been there for a while.

The real estate brokers were looking around thinking, "Oh goodness, now what do we do?" They thought the agent might have known something about the mold or something that could have given rise to a duty to disclose and do more investigation about the mold. So the brokerage got—I don't know if "clever" is the right word—but it got clever and challenged the lawsuit on the basis that the child wasn't their client, and therefore they had no duty to investigate on behalf of the child.

As you can imagine, the trial court didn't like that so much and struggled with the decision but eventually ruled in favor of the brokerage.

The client, the customer, appealed because, as you can imagine, they didn't like that decision one little bit.

The Court of Appeal struggled with this for a little bit too and still ruled in favor of the brokers, saying, "You know, the statutory scheme for doing an investigation and providing a disclosure is specifically laid out in the language of the statute. A broker is to inspect, disclose, and give that disclosure documentation 'to a prospective purchaser.' The minor child wasn't a prospective purchaser. Common law duties and cases have been decided which speak to the duties that a real estate broker owes to the buyer of the real estate, as this couple was; but the child wasn't the buyer."

Thus the Court of Appeal looked at how the complaint had been framed and decided in favor of the real estate brokers and avoided liability because the child wasn't the client.

Should a brokerage take comfort in that?

Yes and no. There's a common law duty to be honest and truthful to everyone involved in a transaction; and in this particular instance, the child wasn't involved "in the transaction." There have been other cases where tangential third parties, and even a subsequent buyer, have been able to reach back and impose liability on a broker that didn't make a disclosure *a transaction earlier* or sometimes even *two* transactions earlier.

The takeaway on this case is—be careful. Here, the real estate broker escaped liability. That will not always be the case.

2 | Getting Paid

A topic that is near and dear to every agent's heart (and every brokerage's too) is "How do we get paid?" You'd think that that would be the easy part. Think again.

One thing that is necessary for a brokerage to have in order to create a legal right to force a client to pay is a written agreement relating to compensation. Sounds fair. But is it— always?

What to Do When a Buyer Breaches?

(Adapted from: Chan v. Tsang, 1 Cal.App.4th 1578)

I'm going to take you back in time again but only to 1992, and we're going to stay in Palo Alto. (Wouldn't it be cool to still have the Model T?)

An agent had a client that was looking to buy some commercial property, so he showed the customer property after property after property. Finally—finally—the customer made an offer on a four million-dollar piece of property. The commission on this one (any agent could do the math in her head) was going to be $100,000. The agent had already mentally spent it way before the deal got closed.

This deal, in fact, never closed. The buyer, for no reason, no stated reason anyway, simply decided not to go forward with the deal and breached the contract.

Now, there was a $20,000 deposit that was put up when the contract was signed—and the seller wanted that twenty grand pursuant to the liquidated damages provision of the contract.

The agent, meanwhile, was over there thinking, "How can I get part of the $20,000? Wait a minute, how can I get my $100,000?"

The buyer refused to sign the cancellation instructions to simply give up the $20,000, so the seller had to file suit. The seller sued the real estate broker—the buyer's real estate broker— too. (That's just adding insult to injury.)

The case marched forward, and the seller won, getting the $20,000 as liquidated damages. The buyer appealed and lost. (Sometimes, there is justice …)

The real estate broker, who had filed a cross-complaint against the buyer, was dismissed in the claim by the seller but kept the claim going against the buyer for the $100,000 commission.

Now, according to the terms of the purchase agreement, the seller was supposed to pay the real estate commission from the proceeds of the sale. The broker for the buyer was hired by the buyer, so it wasn't a dual agency.

Again, for those not familiar with how the industry works: a brokerage can represent a seller, a buyer, or both. It frequently happens where one agent in a brokerage represents a seller, and a different agent, the buyer. But since the agents work for the same broker, the "brokerage" is deemed to represent both the seller and the buyer. When the brokerage represents both, it is called a "dual agency."

When the real estate broker—the buyer's broker—sued the buyer, the buyer tried to defend against the claim by arguing, "The deal didn't close, so there's no commission due from the seller."

That approach didn't work because it was the buyer who breached the deal.

So then the buyer responded, "But wait, but wait, according to the listing agreement itself—it says that if the buyer breaches the contract, the seller is only responsible to pay the real estate broker 50% of the amount of the money that the seller actually collects from the buyer up to the maximum amount of the commission. And since the seller only got twenty grand, that means the most that the broker can get is $10,000—half of the twenty grand."

And the trial court agreed.

As you can imagine, that made the buyer's broker unhappy. And don't you know, the broker appealed saying, "This just doesn't seem right."

The Court of Appeal agreed with the broker and said, "You're right. You get the $100,000."

Now, it was the buyer's turn to scream bloody murder—"How come? How come? The listing agreement says that in the event of a default by the buyer, and that's me, and I'll even agree that I defaulted under the purchase agreement, but the most the broker can get is half of the amount that the seller collected. If the seller only got $20,000, that's $10,000. What's the problem here?"

And here's what the Court of Appeal concluded: "The listing agreement says that the broker can get *from the seller* half of what the seller collects, but the listing agreement doesn't say anything about what the broker can get from *the buyer*; and in this case, because the buyer interfered with the transaction between the buyer and the seller which caused the broker to lose the $100,000 commission, that's the amount that the broker is entitled to receive *from the buyer*."

The court said that it's much like the broker was a third party beneficiary under the purchase agreement between the buyer and the seller; and as a result, it was intended for the broker to collect the full $100,000 on the commission. Thus, when the buyer breached that agreement, the buyer inherited the obligation to pay the broker the full amount that the broker would otherwise have received.

Not a bad day's work for the real estate brokerage.

Does it always work out that way? Oh, hell no. In fact, let's go back again to Silicon Valley for an example of when it doesn't work out so well.

But I Brought In a Full Price Offer!

(Adapted from: Real Pro v. Smith, 203 Cal.App.4th 1215)

All these cases seem to be about money, about making money, or about collecting a commission that the brokerage earned … Or had it?

Here's a case where there was a $17 million-dollar listing and an agent with a client that wanted that property. So the agent and buyer made an offer, an all-cash offer, for the full $17 million. The buyer's agent happily presented it to the listing agent, and it went to the seller—who then made a counteroffer … for $19.5 million.

The buyer's agent sat there wondering what had just happened. After all, hadn't he just made a full price, all-cash offer? All of the terms of the listing agreement had been met because the listing agreement said that the seller would accept, and I quote, "$17 million in cash or such other price and terms that are acceptable to the seller."

"$17 million in cash or such other price and terms as are acceptable."

Now, I've been in this business a long time, and what I've always understood that phrase to mean is "$17 million dollars or some lesser amount or other terms acceptable to the seller." If I had brought in a full price, all-cash offer for the listing, I'd be thinking that deal is done. So did the broker in this case, right up until the seller said, "No."

As you might guess, the broker sued for the commission. It was a big commission! I'd have sued too.

And the trial court decided, "No."

And the broker appealed, as I would have done as well.

The Court of Appeal sided with the seller and also concluded, "No."

The appellate justices, far more picky than my sixth grade English teacher, explained, "You know, there's not a comma in that listing agreement that says '$17 million dollars or such price and terms as acceptable,' but we're going to infer that there is. And we are not going to insert the phrase 'or some lesser amount' because—think of the chaos that could result if we did. After all, what if you had five people that all walked in and said, 'Here's $17 million dollars all-cash.' Would the seller have to pay five different commissions?"

The broker countered, "No, you pay the commission to the one who came in first or the one that was accepted of those five because that's when the sale would happen." The Court of Appeal decided, "No, we're not buying that argument."

So this broker, who procured a $17 million all-cash offer, got screwed out of that commission. Was that fair?

That's a tough call. (And remember, I'm a broker too; when I first read this case, I mentally spent the commission myself!)

The question boiled down to: If you're the seller and you get an offer, are you automatically bound to sell your real estate just because someone makes you an offer?

Clearly the answer there is no. But, on the flipside of that, if a seller executes a listing agreement and says, "I am offering this property for sale … at this price, on these terms," and someone meets that price and those terms, shouldn't the seller now be bound? Or is the seller merely inviting offers on property that it might sell? Does a listing merely mean that the seller may or may not accept whatever offer comes in, even a full price one?

That's what the Court of Appeal said a listing was—merely an invitation to have people bring offers to a seller that the seller did not necessarily need to accept.

I don't make this stuff up. I only write about it.

I think the court got this one wrong. There are, in the world of personal property (think: manufacturing equipment) things called Merchant Firm Offers, where, when a seller offers up a piece of equipment at a certain price and a buyer says, "Yup, I'll take that," the seller can't back away from the deal. It is not a novel concept. Here, where the seller hired a brokerage to sell the property and made it available to the marketplace, at a certain list price—set by the seller—I think the seller ought to have been bound by a buyer who says, "Yup, I'll take that."

But I'm not on the court of appeal.

3 | The Forms ARE Your Friend (Most of the Time)

Agents and brokers need to study the forms they use. Everyone needs to be careful about how they are used. Know them backward and forward. But, even then, you must be careful. Really, really careful.

From the counter intuitive "counter-counter" offer result, I'd like to take you to another case where knowing the forms and how to use them could have made a seller an easy three million dollars. But, because the seller (or the agent) didn't know how to manipulate the forms to their advantage, they lost out. Well, that, plus the court didn't like the way the seller was playing fast and loose with the buyer.

Giving Trailer Trash a Whole New Meaning

(Adapted from: Rutherford Holdings v. Plaza Del Rey,
223 Cal.App.4th 221)

This is a case where somebody had more money than sense—or just got greedy. Or maybe a little of both.

This one revolves around a mobile home park (think: "trailer trash")—everybody's favorite real estate subject. Except this mobile home park is in Sunnyvale, California, the epicenter of the Silicon Valley. (Seems we just can't get out of Santa Clara County, can we?)

The seller of this park decided it was time to cash in and listed it for $110 million. It got an offer, with a three million-dollar "non-refundable" deposit. This owner thought it was in great shape. It was going to cash out; all was good.

It turns out that, for a reason that didn't make any sense to me, the seller thought that it would be better for it to not be in contract at one period of time when the property was being reassessed because it thought that the assessor would reassess the property based on the contract purchase price rather than the then market value-appraisal price. So the seller convinced the buyer, who had already gotten two extensions to close escrow, to let the next extension lapse, with the assurance that the buyer would be able to come back into contract and buy the property.

So that's what the buyer agreed to do.

Some months later, when the buyer was ready to move forward, the seller said, "Yeah, well, we've decided not to sell after all. Oh, and by the way, since you didn't close escrow when you were supposed to in the first place, we're keeping the three million-dollar 'non-refundable' deposit. Thanks!"

As you might guess, the buyer was a little unhappy about the seller's position on that, both because the buyer wanted to continue the purchase and absolutely because the buyer believed it had not forfeited the $3 million bucks. So it sued.

The Court of Appeal treated this something like a law school exam, you know—offer, acceptance, consideration, counter-offer. Did it lapse or did it not lapse? What happens to the "time is of the essence provision"—is it invoked or is it impliedly waived? All those kinds of things came up.

And here's where the Court of Appeal landed: "If neither party performs the contract on the closing date, the contract is deemed terminated; it's void." The court then noted that neither party had breached the agreement. And, it reasoned, "Since there is no breach, there is no liquidated damage amount that can be imposed upon the buyer."

With regard to that fancy-pants, non-refundability provision, the court stated, "Since there is no contract because it's been voided, then there is no non-refundability provision in a contract that would trigger the loss of that deposit by a buyer."

At the end of the day, the ruling was that there had been no breach of contract because neither party performed to trigger the performance of the other party and the contract had lapsed; therefore, the deposit had to be returned.

So here's what that smarty-pants seller in Sunnyvale could have done and earned three million bucks: tendered performance.

All the seller needed to do was go into the title company on the day of the scheduled closing, execute the Grant Deed, sign the escrow instructions, and give the purchaser notice of the seller's performance. By doing that, the seller would have "tendered performance," the buyer would have been in breach, and the deposit would then have been forfeited. There was no way the buyer was going to perform on time. It was snarky to try to keep the money without at least giving lip service to honoring the contract.

Here's a case where the seller outsmarted themselves by jumping the gun and failing to read their own contract. Well, that plus they got greedy. That's why the Court of Appeal said, "No."

So what's the takeaway on something like this?

Many, many times, we are presented with a scenario where the seller wants to back out of the deal or the buyer wants to push the seller into performing the deal. We're asked, "What does the client need to do in order to trigger that performance?" The answer, often, is "tender performance."

We recently had a case of a property in Tahoe with exactly the same scenario, and by tendering performance, by delivering the deed to the escrow company, the seller was able to push the buyer into walking away from the contract, so that the seller could sell it, for more, to someone else.

As a real estate representative for either the seller or the buyer, you need to be aware of the "tender trap" because it can equally work to your advantage or it can work to the other side's advantage. Be very careful. Pay very close attention.

Here's a case where I think the brokerage got screwed, because the form was used "incorrectly."

Form Over Substance

(Adapted from: Roth v. Malson, 67 Cal.App.4th 552)

This next story, frankly, burns my bacon. It's a case that puts form over substance.

A buyer made an offer to buy property for $41,600, all-cash, close in 30 days. The seller made a counteroffer. Instead of $41,600 and close in 30 days, the seller wanted $44,000. The seller still wanted to close in 30 days. So the seller filled out the form called "Counteroffer" and submitted it to the buyer.

Now, the buyer's original offer was dated November 2, and the counteroffer was dated November 6. So the buyer, instead of marking the box that said "Acceptance," wanted to be really precise and checked the box that said, "Counter counter," and wrote "$44,000, close of Escrow to be December 6," which was 30 days from the November 6 date of the counteroffer.

In between the time when the seller wrote the counter offer and the buyer sent back the counter-counter offer, the seller changed his mind and decided not to sell the real estate at all.

The buyer, thinking he had a deal, sued for specific performance, arguing, "I want this property. I'm going to give you the $44,000 that you wanted. It's all-cash. And I'm going to close in 30 days."

The trial court said, "No." And the buyer said, "Baloney!" and appealed—and lost.

The Court of Appeal said this: "It's true that *the substance* of the 'counter to counter' didn't change at all any of the material terms of the counteroffer. The buyer agreed to $44,000 and agreed to close in 30 days. Since the counter was dated November 6, the buyer's specific date of December 6 for the closing was still the very same 30 days. But, because the buyer checked the box that said, 'Counter counter,' and signed the agreement there, that was not an 'unqualified acceptance' of the counteroffer." Therefore, the seller got away with cancelling the deal—even though the buyer accepted all of the terms of the counteroffer.

As a real estate agent or as a real estate broker, what do you learn from this case?

Normally I would tell an agent that "the form is your friend;" that an agent should use the forms and not try to create something on their own; and that an agent should be incredibly careful when writing counteroffers—because the law of unintended consequences means an agent will get punished for whatever the good deed is the agent is trying to do.

If a brokerage has in-house counsel or a risk-management department, or if there's a lawyer for the buyer or the seller, the agent should direct their client to the lawyers when dealing with changes to the purchase agreement forms. And—no, this is not the full employment for lawyers' speech. (Although, if you think you might need a lawyer to look stuff over or give brilliantly intelligent cautionary advice on what to do or not to do, give us a call. That is, after all, what *we* do.)

This case is a really good lesson in how trying to do the right thing but checking the wrong box can have disastrous consequences.

This is one of the reasons that the California Association of Realtors ® has designed and made all kinds of forms available to both commercial and residential brokers who are members of its association. (Other companies have similar products, so this is NOT a pitch for CAR ...) No matter which form you use, it is, generally, best to use a form. A form can be your friend.

4 | No Good Deed Goes Unpunished

"The court finds that you have not yet been punished for some of your good deeds."

The forms are not the only thing a real estate agent and brokerage should pay attention to. There are any number of opportunities in the life of a transaction where someone can slip up. So far we've talked about contract formation and protecting the right to get paid. What about after a contract has been formed? What about paying attention to the other details, like the myriad disclosures a brokerage has to make to a client?

Here's an instance of an agent thinking he knew what he was talking about that went terribly, terribly, wrong.

Stateless Russians

(Adapted from: Salahutin v. Alcantara,
24 Cal.App.4th 555)

I want to take you back in time again, to 1917—to the Russian Revolution, where the Czar is slaughtering people left and right. Anybody that can get out of Russia is getting out of Russia. They go to China. They go to Japan. They go to anywhere in Europe. One particular couple ended up going to Korea where they were deemed "stateless people."

Stateless people couldn't buy property, couldn't vote, and had no citizenship. That's a very, very difficult way to live.

Eventually, the couple was able to get to America, and they ended up in San Jose. Their overriding goal in life was to make sure that their children were never stateless, were never property-less. And so, when it came time for them to buy real estate, they wanted to be sure that the property they bought could be subdivided, so their son and their daughter would receive ownership of real estate in their own right.

They sought out a real estate agent to help them find just that kind of property, and they landed on someone in Hillsborough, which, by the way, isn't a bad place to find lots to subdivide. They told the agent exactly what they wanted and exactly *why* they wanted it. The agent was very clear about the importance of subdivide-ability for these clients. The clients told the agent there was no hurry. They were willing to wait as long as it took until they found just the right piece of property.

Lo and behold, shortly after they met, the real estate agent saw an ad in the multiple listing service: "One-plus acre."

The fact that the property was "one-plus" acre was important because the agent knew that in order to subdivide land in Hillsborough, the original piece had to be at least one acre in size. So this property fit the bill.

The couple made an offer. They closed escrow. It was all good.

During the escrow, the agent met the couple on the property, and as they were looking at the boundary fences, the agent noted, "That fence over there on the south side, that's the borderline." He stuck his thumb out, explaining, "Yeah, I've eyeballed it. This is an acre. Says so on the MLS too."

A couple of years later, when the next-door neighbors did a survey and moved that back fence about 10 feet to the true property line—it turned out that the size of the lot the broker sold these folks was 0.998 of an acre—two one-hundredths short of that full acre and thus, maybe not subdividable.

These clients were unhappy and sued the broker for fraud, for negligence, and for misrepresentation. The broker relied on the Multiple Listing Service, the information from the sellers, the seller's agent, and everyone else that was involved in the deal.

And the court said, "Too bad."

Because the real estate broker representing the buyers said that he'd eyeballed the property and thus opined that it was an acre-plus, the agent was responsible for that representation as one of fact, not merely opinion. Because the agent eyeballed the fence and declared, "Yeah, that's the boundary line," without checking or without saying that he hadn't verified that it was indeed the boundary line, the agent was responsible for the misrepresentation.

Innocently made or not, passing on a representation that an agent has not verified is called "constructive fraud." Whether it's innocently done or not, if an agent passes it on, the agent owns it and is responsible for it if it's wrong.

So what's the lesson to be learned from this?

Don't say what you don't know.

If a fact hasn't been checked, say so. If this agent had done that, there likely wouldn't have been liability; but because the agent adopted the others' representations, it became the agent's representation.

While passing on opinions of acreage, or square footage, are things that regularly get agents and brokerages in trouble, those are not the only kinds of representations that can, or do.

5 | Doing the Right Thing

Julia Morgan

We all know that an agent's job, especially when representing a seller, is to put a property in the best light possible. "Staging" a home is a normal part of the selling process nowadays. In fact, there are companies set up to do just that.

So where is the line that someone shouldn't cross when it comes to describing the attributes of a property? Saying it is "adorned with lovely sunlight through the bay windows" might be OK if there are, in fact, bay windows. It probably isn't OK to say if the only window is in a lightwell between two four-story Victorian buildings. Even then, though, a buyer can see that the description is a little puffing. And a little puffing, a little exaggeration, a little flowery hyperbole is OK.

When does it cross the line? Here's an example of what is NOT OK.

Did She or Didn't She? Only Her Godchild Knows for Sure

(Adapted from: Jue v. Smiser, 23 Cal.App.4th 312)

This next story has to do with an April Fools' Day joke gone bad. Actually, it wasn't a joke.

The property, listed on April 1, was a darling little house in the Oakland Hills that the real estate broker described as "an authenticated Julia Morgan design."

Now, for those of you who don't know, Julia Morgan was a really famous architect here in California from back in the early '20s—so famous, in fact, that she's revered by architects around the state, including the architect who read about the house in an article published in the *San Francisco Chronicle* about a week after the listing.

That architect rushed on over to the Oakland Hills to look at the house and made an offer— Bang!—on the spot. Full price.

How come? He wanted a Julia Morgan house. He wanted to be able to say that he lived in a Julia Morgan house.

All was good, until it came time for deciding how he was going to pay for it.

He wanted to make his purchase of the house contingent upon the sale of his current house, but the real estate broker told him, "That's not such a good idea." After all, he might be undercut; someone else could come in, without that kind of a contingency, and be able to buy the house out from under him. So he swallowed hard and decided he'd go ahead and list his house for sale, using the same real estate agent because, well, that just made life convenient for everybody.

So the real estate agent went ahead, took the listing, and within a month, had it sold.

This was really good news for the architect.

Here they were, now just two days away from the close of escrow to buy the Julia Morgan property, sitting in a title insurance company office with the real estate broker, who handed the architect an addendum that read, "By the way, there are no plans at City Hall that verified this is indeed a Julia Morgan-designed home."

The architect and his wife paused, for quite some time, just looking at the document and the agent. Finally, the architect asked, "Well, how come? Your earlier documentation says it's an authenticated Julia Morgan." The real estate broker confessed that she wasn't "sure" and wanted to make clear that the architect knew she wasn't sure.

The papers did not get signed that day.

For the next couple of days, the architect and his wife scrambled around. They spoke with an author who had written a book about Julia Morgan, who told them that she was convinced that it *was* indeed a Julia Morgan design.

The architect had also reached out to Julia Morgan's goddaughter (who, apparently had made her life's work the documenting the projects that her godmother had done).

The goddaughter told the architect that she *didn't* have anything that conclusively proved that this *was* indeed a Julia Morgan-designed house.

The architect found himself between a rock and a hard place. If he didn't sign off on the deal, he'd be homeless; after all, he'd not get the house in Oakland, and he'd already sold his previous house.

Confronted with a no-win scenario, the architect signed the documents and closed the deal—then shortly thereafter sued the real estate broker for fraud—for making a misrepresentation that the house was an authenticated Julia Morgan when in fact there was no such authentication.

The broker lost, and the case went up on appeal. The broker explained, "Well, there's no way that the architect could have relied on the representation because, prior to the close of escrow, the architect was advised that the broker wasn't sure."

"Indeed," the broker continued, "the architect went out and verified the home's status with the author and the goddaughter, so the architect had full knowledge of the inconclusive nature of the claim of being a Julia Morgan design prior to closing the escrow. Therefore, when the architect closed, the architect did it with full knowledge of the uncertainty. There was no reliance on a misrepresentation by the broker at all."

Once again, our illustrious court of appeal said, "Yeah, ah— no."(Wouldn't it be cool if a court of appeal actually wrote something like that—just once?)

What the court did say was that the "reliance" existed at the time that the architect made the offer, not at the time of the close of escrow. And that was enough.

So what's the takeaway?

If an agent is going to describe a unique characteristic of a property, the agent must be sure it's right because that's not the time to play April Fools'.

There are other kinds of things that a brokerage can also do to get in trouble. Like, say, making or arranging loans for clients.

I'm not talking about institutional loans (though a loan broker has plenty of opportunities to get in trouble there too …) but rather "hard money" loans, the kind you get from private individuals.

"Hard money" loans are regulated much more severely now, thanks to the changes in regulations arising from the Great Recession, and this next story is about a loan that was made before those regulations came into effect. The point is still valid, as it pertains to the rate of interest that can be charged on a loan, even a private-lender hard money loan.

Can I Borrow (… or Steal) a Little Money?

(Adapted from: Bock v. California Capital Loans,
216 Cal.App.4th 264)

This story is about usury. Some of you may not know what usury is, so give me another 10 seconds to explain.

There's a concept in the law that says, "While it's okay to make a loan, you can't charge too much interest. If you do, it's usurious; it's not allowed." And California sets that interest rate, as a matter of law, at 10%.

Now, there are exceptions to the usury law where you can actually charge more than 10%, and that's where real estate brokers get a lot of friends because if a loan is made or arranged by a real estate broker, for someone else, in expectation of compensation, the interest rate on that loan can be anything that the market will bear. In this case, a real estate broker arranged a loan, and the rate of interest was 15%.

Of course, the borrower defaulted on that loan, and the lender foreclosed on the real estate. The borrower sued to have the foreclosure set aside and to get the real estate back. That's when it began to get interesting.

How come? Because the borrower said the loan was usurious.

The borrower's claim was that the broker who "made or arranged the loan" was also the trustee of the trust that was the lender; and if the broker was also the lender, the borrower said, then that's not a loan made or arranged "by another." The borrower also noted that the broker did not collect a real estate commission. So, the borrower claimed, if the loan was not done "for compensation" and if it wasn't "made or arranged for another" in the expectation of compensation, the loan was usurious.

The trial court, perhaps not sympathetic to the defaulting borrower, granted the real estate broker's motion to dismiss the case. The borrower appealed. The Court of Appeal looked at these two issues carefully.

First, with regard to whether or not the loan was made or arranged "for another," the court said that it was *the trust* that was the lender, and the broker was merely the trustee of the trust. Just as a trustee's personal assets cannot be used to pay a creditor of the trust because it's the trust that owes the debt, not the trustee, so here the trust was the lender and as such was going to get the benefit of the collection of interest on the loan, not the broker in his capacity as trustee of the trust.

With regard to whether or not the broker received compensation for arranging the loan, the Court of Appeal said "compensation" didn't have to be in the form of the payment of "money" and that the trustee of the trust, the broker that arranged the loan, could receive the benefit from the trust and payment by the trust when the trust dissolved. This, the court said, was the "expectation of future compensation" sufficient to constitute "compensation" for making the loan.

Thus the trust was able to foreclose upon the property.

There have been other cases where usurious loans have been made or arranged by a broker who *hasn't* received compensation or where the broker has made the loan *himself* and even paid himself a commission when doing that; and in both those instances, the loan was found to be usurious.

So if you find yourself in a scenario where you are making or arranging private money loans for someone else, you should check to be sure that you are actually "right on the money" (I couldn't resist the pun) with regard to making or arranging, for another, with the expectation of compensation.

While helping others buy or sell property, or even arrange loans, is the typical thing an agent does for a customer, every now and then the agent wants to do a little work for themselves. After all, they know real estate pretty well. A smart agent can smell a good deal. Why not gobble up a piece every now and then?

That's OK to do. There's nothing that says an agent can't buy property for their own account. Well ...

6 | Doing the Wrong Thing

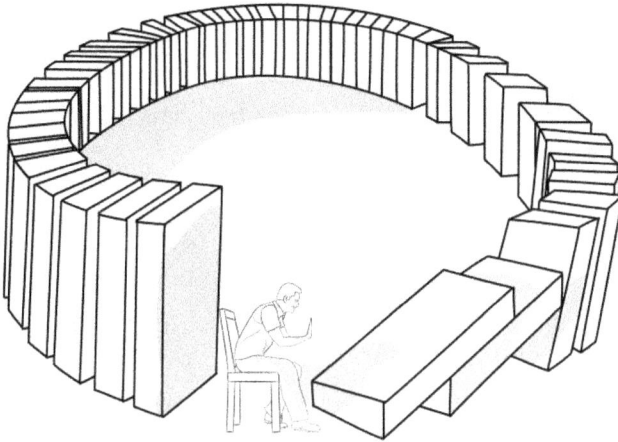

Oh, what a tangled web we weave ...

More than one California court has observed that the creativity of humans is nearly limitless, especially when it comes to money, especially when cheating someone out of it. A real estate investment has often proven to be a successful way to make a buck. Sometimes it can be a fast buck (see: foreclosure flippers.) Sometimes, somebody tries to make a fast buck faster. That is when ... issues? ... can arise.

Liar, Liar, Pants on Fire

(Adapted from: Ward v. Taggart, 51 Cal.2d 736)

The story begins with Bill, who had been looking to buy some real estate to develop down in Los Angeles. He'd been working with his broker, LeRoy, for months to try to find just the right piece—a big enough piece, in just the right location—all that good stuff. And poor LeRoy was struggling with coming up with a property that would work for Bill.

LeRoy was bemoaning this difficult project to one of his buddies, Marshall, down at the country club. Marshall, ever the helpful guy, said, "But LeRoy, I know just the piece for you."

"Really?"

"Yeah, it's the 70 acres down here that Sunset Oil is selling. I've got it listed. You ought to go take a look."

And sure enough, after LeRoy got in the car and drove down there to take a look, he came away thinking this might be just exactly what Bill was looking for.

There was one thing though. LeRoy noticed a sign that had a different real estate broker's name on it: "For sale. By: Jim Jones."

So LeRoy called up Marshall and explained, "We like it. Bill wants to make an offer, but what's the deal with Jim Jones?"

"Oh don't worry about that," Marshall told him. "That's an old listing. I've got it listed with Sunset Oil, and you should bring any offers through me. We got you covered."

So LeRoy and Bill worked it out. They came up with an offer price—$4,000 an acre. They submitted it to Marshall, and he took it to Sunset Oil. A few days later, Marshall came back with a counteroffer, explaining that Sunset Oil wanted $5,000 an acre, and they wanted Bill to increase the amount of the down payment to 50%, all-cash. So Bill and LeRoy talked about it, and Bill decided, "Okay, I'll do it."

LeRoy amended the offer and submitted it. Sunset Oil accepted, and all was good. A few days later Bill brought in a bunch of money to Marshall for the down payment.

When it came time for the closing papers to be signed, Bill and LeRoy went to the title company for sign off. They noticed the papers didn't show Sunset Oil as the seller. It was Marshall's partner, Jordan, identified as the seller.

So they asked Marshall, "What's that all about?"

"Oh, it's part of the fixing up of the listing agreement stuff with the other broker, and we're taking care of some tax problems. It's all just pro-forma. Don't worry about it."

Accepting that answer, Bill signed off and away he went. The deal closed, Bill got the property, and he was feeling all warm and fuzzy inside.

Once Bill started doing some entitlement processing to get the property ready for development, he found out that Sunset Oil really was the seller, not this Jordan person. And he found out that *Marshall* had bought the property for $4,000 an acre from Sunset Oil and re-sold it to him at $5,000 an acre. Bill learned that Marshall had made up all of this business about the exclusive listing belonging to him and that there was no tax problem requiring the papers to be set up "differently." What really got Bill's goat was that he discovered Marshall had used *his* down payment money as Marshall's down payment in the intervening deal! Marshall had just outright snookered Bill. Marshall bought the property from Sunset and re-sold it to Bill. For a $1,000 per acre "markup."

Well, that made Bill a little unhappy. I guess it would make anybody a little unhappy. So he sued Marshall to get his money back—his extra $1,000 an acre; and he won. The court awarded punitive damages against Marshal as well.

And Marshall appealed!

Marshall thought that the judgment was unfair because, after all, the property was worth $5,000 an acre. Marshall argued that the law stated that the damages for "fraud" was the difference in the value of the real estate from what you thought it was worth and what it was really worth. Marshall claimed there was no damage to Bill, because the property was worth what Bill paid, at $5,000 an acre.

And the court said, "Nope. We're not going to let you get away with that."

It would have unjustly enriched Marshall had he been able to get away with selling the property without disclosing that he was flipping it to Bill. So the court imposed what's called a "constructive trust" over the proceeds of the sale from Marshall to Bill and made Marshall give Bill the extra $1,000 an acre.

The court also made Marshall responsible for all the real estate commissions payable in the transaction; and, again, Marshall appealed.

Marshall said, "You know, the award in the trial court requiring me to pay all of the commissions and everything is unfair. Bill would have had to pay a commission no matter what. So I, Marshall, shouldn't have to pay those commissions. Bill should."

And, again, the court said, "No."

The justices believed it appropriate that part of the penalty that imposed upon Marshall should be *all* of the costs, including the commissions that would have otherwise been paid anyway because—and this is the part where, oh, adding insult to injury comes in—as the court said to Marshal, "Bill might not have had to have paid all of those commissions or at least not that much; and it would be too speculative to try to consider how much Bill would have actually paid if the deal had been legitimate. So, we're just going to let you pay all of those fees and costs."

Ouchie.

We all know that commissions are payable on a deal. And we know that, almost always, those costs are built into the price the buyer pays for the property. Calling it "speculative" ... well, let's just say the court might have had blinders on that day.

And it proves the point that no bad deed will go unpunished. Sometimes no good deed goes unpunished. But in this case, Marshall got everything he deserved; and the court needed to work it around a little bit to come up with the appropriate theory.

You see, Marshall was not a fiduciary to Bill. He wasn't Bill's agent. So a typical "breach of fiduciary duty" claim wouldn't have worked.

There are other circumstances where a real estate broker can get, and has gotten, into trouble by doing a similar thing to a client. For instance, where the real estate broker's customer makes a low bid, and the real estate broker knows that the property is worth more so makes a higher bid and cuts the client out of the deal. Or where a real estate broker has a client working under a buyer's representation agreement and the buyer is relying on the real estate broker to find a certain type of property for the client; the broker then buys something so that the broker can make a profit and resell it to that client.

Once you've established the agency relationship, you have a fiduciary duty to put the client's interests ahead of yours. It's okay to flip a property and to make a profit. It's not okay to do it secretly, and it's not okay to cheat a client out of the profit that the client would have made had you introduced that property to the client.

How else can an agent/broker get in trouble? Oh, the ways are as varied as the imagination of an individual, or the courts.

One theme remains pretty constant throughout. If an agent knows of a problem, the agent must tell the client about it. But can an agent pretend not to see a problem? Can an agent ignore obvious signs that, if the agent probed—even just a little bit—would reveal a much bigger problem? We all know the phrase "plausible deniability." Can an agent avail herself of that veil? And, just exactly what duty is there on an agent to investigate to see if there is a problem or not? I mean, really, does an agent have to call a structural engineer to investigate every little crack in the sidewalk? Does an agent have to crawl around in the foundations of a building to see if there is a "problem" there? The attic? Is an agent supposed to be an expert in roofing, plumbing, electrical, or structural components?

No. But ...

Slip Sliding Away ...

(Adapted from: Easton v. Strassburger,
152 Cal.App.3d 90)

It's well known, now, in California that in a residential real estate transaction, the broker has an obligation to conduct a reasonably competent, diligent visual inspection of the accessible areas of a property and to disclose the material facts that that investigation reveals. That has not always been the case.

Where did the obligation come from?

I want you to come back in time with me to 1984. You are the purchaser of this wonderful house overlooking the Bay Area. It's a four-bridge view. It's got a nice slope. It's a house with a pretty deck and a guest cottage to boot. You can sit out there with your margaritas and watch the sun set over the Golden Gate, day after day, after day—because the fog is way up in Berkeley, and this house *isn't* in the fog belt. It is the house of your dreams. You buy it up, and you are just happy as hell.

One of the things you want to do is build a pool, so you start excavating. As soon as the trencher digs the third scoop, half the hillside falls away. That beautiful deck starts to slide down the hill. The foundation of the house is undermined, and now you are looking at hundreds of thousands of dollars in repair bills. This ... does not make you happy.

What do you do?

You find out who knew this might happen and when they knew. And why the hell they didn't tell you before you bought this piece-of-crap property!

"Massive earth movement" is the way the slide was described in the court files. And it turns out it wasn't the first time this property had been subject to "massive earth movement." It turns out that 3 or 4 years before, there had been "a minor slide" and that about 9 months after that, there had been—

well, something other than a minor slide, a slide where a hole 8 to 10 feet deep—and 50 to 60 feet wide—had appeared in the middle of this property.

It turns out that the house had been built on fill and that the fill hadn't been compacted correctly. When sued for the damages the buyer suffered, the question became whether or not the real estate agents knew, or should have known, about the defect in this property.

Until this case went to trial, and then appeal, the law had been that a real estate broker was responsible for disclosing the things that the broker *actually* knew about the property and nothing more. Here, it was proven that the broker *did not know* that there had been landslides or slumpage on this property.

"Time out," said the court. "Did the broker have reason to suspect that there would be landslide or slumpage problems? Did the broker do an investigation—any investigation—that would have triggered an obligation to find out about the landslide problem?"

And thus the questions began.

The court found that the agents had done some looking around and made some disclosures. One of the things that the agents identified was that netting had been placed on part of the property. And another of the agents knew that there had been erosion problems on land near there and helpfully noted that "fill" sometimes had erosion problems.

One of the agents who had been to the house said, "You know, the guest house next to where the pool was going to go, had a sloping floor." The other agent said, "Well, sometimes sloping floors can mean that there's a foundation problem." Even though no one agent involved in the transaction had knowledge of all of those different pieces, the "brokerage" was deemed to, as the overall entity.

Adopting the phrase one of the agents used in a deposition, the court decided that there were "red flags" that could have indicated a potential problem. Once aware of the potential problem, the court said that it would have been prudent for the brokerage to advise the customer to get a soils engineer to come out and investigate.

When confronted with such a "potential problem," the court explained that the broker had a duty to take that information, which the broker didn't know with certainty was a problem, and advise the client to do further investigation.

This was a massive shift in the level of responsibility that would be due from a brokerage to a customer. So what did the court use to hang its hat on in order to impose this duty?

The real estate trade association!

You know, trade associations, like unions, can be good things sometimes; and they can be bad things sometimes.

The National Association of Realtors is a trade association that a licensed salesperson or broker can join. It's voluntary. Not all licensees are members of the trade association.

Love it or hate it, the NAR had (and still has) a "code of ethics" in existence at the time. In that code of ethics, it ("it" being the trade association based out of Washington, DC) said that a broker had "an affirmative obligation to discover adverse factors that might affect the value or desirability of the property" and that "performing a reasonably competent visual inspection" was one of the things that a broker *should* do under the code of ethics ... of the *trade association*.

The Court of Appeal said, "That's good enough for us..." and created the *legal duty* of a real estate broker to conduct that reasonably competent, diligent visual inspection of accessible areas and to disclose what that investigation would find.

From that point, it was easy for the Court to say that netting on landfilled areas would suggest that a geologic survey would be prudent. Of course the brokerage in this case hadn't done that. There had never been an obligation to do so—before this case.

The broker got nailed for the costs of rehabilitation of this property because they didn't suggest that the buyer conduct further investigations, even after the agents saw what they thought of as "red flags."

So what's the takeaway on this one?

Lots of times, an agent will walk into a house and see a crack in the ceiling, white efflorescence on the side of a garage wall, or some water stains near a foundation.

Are those red flags sufficient to give the agent, as the professional, an obligation to suggest that the client get additional investigations? Absolutely!

There is no such thing as a perfect house. And so when you see on a seller disclosure statement that the door sticks in winter, it's because it's warped and not square—that could be because the foundation is sliding away; or it could be because the house has settled (like most 100-year-old Victorians are wont to do).

To protect itself, a brokerage should always advise a customer to have additional inspections by competent professionals done for each and every area of concern.

OK, so now we have learned that an agent has to do a reasonably competent and diligent visual inspection of accessible areas of a property. (I always remark at that language. The inspection doesn't have to be a thorough one, just a "reasonably" competent one. But I digress ...)

If an agent is aware of "something" that might be a "red flag," what is the extent of the disclosure that has to be made? That will be answered in our next story.

Water, Water, Everywhere

(Adapted from: Sweat v. Holister, 37 Cal.App.4th 603)

I now introduce you to … the sweet young couple who just bought their first house.

They were just excited as can be. They saved up. They scrimped. They searched and searched and searched to find just the right place; and they finally found it.

You know how it goes. The real estate agent took them through and showed them the house." Here is a bedroom. Here is a kitchen." Yada, yada, yada.

The agent gave them this massive disclosure package and part of that included this thing called a Natural Hazard Disclosure Statement. It contained a bunch of stuff—an earthquake zone disclosure and other disclosures about military ordnance zones and airport noise zones. There was even one that said, "Be careful of golf balls if you're near a golf course."

Of course, part of it also talked about flood zones. The agent disclosed that the property was in a flood zone because, well, it was. The agent didn't say anything more about all those disclosures.

Well, it turned out that not only was the property in a flood zone, but what that meant was that if any part of the property was damaged or destroyed, the sweet young couple would not be able to repair or rebuild it. So basically, they learned (oh—after the fact—of course) what they had just bought was a house—but never the ability to fix it.

Wow. That's not what they bargained for.

So they sued the real estate broker for non-disclosure. They claimed that the house was a non-conforming use inside this floodplain and that this important fact had not been disclosed to them.

Another trial ... another appeal.

The Court of Appeal again was found wrestling with the issue of extent of required disclosure. It was, after all, an evolving area of the law. There are balancing considerations. One instinctively wants to protect the sweet young couple buying their first house or anybody buying a house for that matter. But the question came down to a defining of the legal duty the real estate broker owed with respect to the extent of the disclosure that's made. Here, the real estate broker disclosed that the property was in a flood zone but didn't disclose what that meant. Was that enough?

The Court of Appeal here decided, "Yes."

The legal ramifications of being in a flood zone were outside of the scope of the disclosure requirement of the real estate agent in this case. And so the sweet young couple got their house that they couldn't rebuild or repair; and the real estate broker had no liability.

Was it the right decision?

You know, there are cases that say that the real estate broker has an obligation to make sure that the client understands the import of the material facts related to a property disclosed to the client, and there are cases that say that the broker doesn't have any obligation to disclose the legal ramifications of such facts.

I don't know if I would agree with the Court of Appeal on this one.

The better course of valor, in my opinion, is to make sure that the clients understand what is being disclosed to them. Later cases have shown this to be true, especially if you're the buyer's representative, because the fiduciary duties there are much broader than merely conducting a visual inspection, like those for a listing agent.

In the continuing saga of disclosures, or non-disclosures, as the case may be, we have the story of yet another "disclosure problem."

Condo Water Problems

(Adapted from: Pagano v. Krohn, 60 Cal.App.4th 1)

This particular story revolves around water problems in condominiums.

The Court of Appeal has noted that condominium construction defect litigation in California is as common as crabgrass. I couldn't agree more. It seems like every time that there's a condominium built, you need to wait, oh, 10 years for the construction defect litigation to have finished and run its course. Every fancy roofline, every gable, every gimble, every door, every balcony, every porch—they're all just waiting for some kind of water intrusion, a flashing problem, or some other kind of construction defect.

And this particular condominium was no different.

In fact, there had been 31 separate instances of notices going out from the homeowner's association with respect to problems in this development. Water-related problems.

Three of the other units had severe water intrusion damage, and the seller of this fourth unit knew of those other three. There was even talk around the condo pool about suing the contractor for construction defects as a result of the water intrusion problems.

The seller put the property on the market and got an offer. After acceptance, the buyer started doing all those inspections she'd been told about. But she got nervous and backed out of the deal; she just wasn't comfortable going down that road. And of course, right after that deal was cancelled, the homeowner's association came out with yet another notice and an assessment, all with respect to suing the contractor for construction defects.

Well, sometimes you get a second bite at the apple, and here, that buyer came back and made another offer. This one was for $5,000 less than the first offer; and the buyer signed an "acknowledgment" that she had been made aware of the lawsuit.

Sometime later, after the close of escrow, don't you know it, the condominium that was purchased also ended up with severe water intrusion problems.

The buyer was unhappy, not only because she had to pay the aforementioned special assessments to the homeowner's association for the litigation but also because now this unit turned out to also have severe water damage.

It came to pass that, during the litigation, the buyer found out that the seller had been aware of, well, efflorescence, a white, powdery, chalky kind of substance, on the garage walls of the unit sold. And that there had been moss, or algae, growing on the outside of one of the garages as well. But no one had disclosed those two "facts."

The buyer, with the aid of hindsight, felt that if those two things had been disclosed, the buyer would have done some additional investigation and discovered the water problem. The buyer believed a fast one had just been pulled.

The broker and the seller countered by saying that those two things, the efflorescence and the moss/algae, were events over a year earlier and that the seller wasn't aware of any significant water intrusion problems and truthfully had answered "No" to that question on the box on the transfer disclosure statement.

The Court of Appeal agreed.

I don't know that if I were a broker, that I would take tremendous comfort from the ruling in this case.

I think that the broker and the seller – were caught dancing in the grey area of "lucky" here. If I had been on the court of appeal, I may have gone the other way.

Who's to say whether or not the efflorescence or the moss is a material fact or not? Sometimes moss just grows because that portion of a house is in the shade more often than anything else, right? We all have or have seen moss growing near downspouts. That doesn't mean that there is a severe water intrusion problem. But in this case, it did indicate a water intrusion problem, or *might* have revealed one, if further investigation had been done.

If it were up to me, I would err on the side of caution. I would disclose the moss and the efflorescence. Let the buyer decide if it's material or not. Don't make that judgment call on the buyer's behalf because, if you do and you are wrong, you'll end up spending a lot more time and money—with me.

Of course, if you point out every little thing, if you never puffed at all, you would end up killing all your deals – just like, you know, lawyers like me.

7 | I've Got to Do <u>What</u>?

Duties, schmooties. A broker has to conduct (say it with me, and it's OK to be a little snarky when you do, especially if you give it a little sing-song attitude)—"a reasonably competent, diligent, visual inspection of accessible areas, and disclose what the inspection reveals." Fine. But once that's done, the agent is *done*. Right? Oh, noooooo. Not by a long shot. Well, not if the agent represents a buyer.

I'm a Good Ol' Country Boy, Just Trying to Get By

(Adapted from: Field v. Century 21, 63 Cal.App.4th 18)

This next story is about a case that is a plaintiff lawyer's dream and a real estate broker's nightmare.

Once upon a time, there was this broker who was responsible for the sale of a 5-acre piece of property just outside the Central Valley. The property had rolling hills, meandering streams, beautiful oak trees, and a house where you could sit on the front porch, rocking back and forth, and just enjoy a summer sunset. The property nearly sold itself.

The broker got an offer to buy and easily closed the deal. It was sweet, all the way around.

After closing the sale, the broker got a preliminary title report—that reflected an easement to the local water district.

Well, the broker knew of the easement ahead of time but hadn't read it and hadn't disclosed the complete scope of the easement to the buyer. Oh, and the broker didn't verify, exactly, down to the square foot, how much acreage there really was and didn't bother to check building permit histories to see if the house was built where it was supposed to be built. But, hey, the property ... was beautiful.

Two years later, the buyer got a surprise. The local water district called to say that the property was in the floodplain;

and not just the property, but that the *house* was built over and into the setback limit of the floodplain. Oh, and then the buyer discovered that the lot wasn't as big a piece of land as the broker thought in the first place either. And that floodplain thing that the district was talking about, the buyer discovered it allowed the district to flood the entire property for overflow—for spill water—including the land where the house was.

The buyer now imagined one morning waking up to floodwater in the living room.

The buyer, unhappy, sued the real estate broker for negligence—for the failure to disclose these, you know, kind of important facts about the property.

California Civil Code section 2079 was designed to define the duties of a real estate broker, acting as the listing agent, which is the person hired by a seller to sell their house.

That listing agent was required to perform a reasonably competent, diligent visual inspection of accessible areas. (Sound familiar? That's because the Legislature codified the holding of an earlier case that imposed that duty upon a broker.) One of the good things about that statute was the 2-year statute of limitations from the day of closing. If a client hadn't made a claim within those 2 years, the client was barred from doing so afterward.

And don't you know it, this buyer made the claim after the 2-year period. So the real estate broker tried to use the statute of limitations to protect herself.

"Not so fast," said the court. "The duties owed by a *listing agent to the seller* may well be statutorily defined and may well get the benefit of that 2-year statute of limitations, but the fiduciary duty owed *by a buyer's representative to the buyer* isn't covered by that statute."

"The buyer's representative," the court said, "has the duty to learn of the material facts that might affect the desirability of the property. They are expected to do the research necessary to be able to advise their client about the value and desirability and characteristics of the property."

"That's what a professional is supposed to do," declared the court. "And this statute of limitations business doesn't apply to a breach of fiduciary duty of a buyer's broker and their client. It only applies to the listing agent's obligation—the statutory obligation to do a reasonably competent, diligent visual inspection."

Holy smokes. What just happened? What's the takeaway on this one?

The "get out of jail card" the Legislature gave a listing agent, with that 2-year statute of limitations, just got pulled.

If a broker represents a buyer, that broker needs to put him/herself in the shoes of the client. S/he needs to be *sure* that the client understands what it is they're getting into. If the client asks a question, almost any question, the broker needs to investigate and get the answer.

If the broker doesn't think the client knows what they're doing, the broker needs to explain it until s/he thinks they do. It's the broker's burden to protect the client.

Now, lest you think that it's only real estate brokers picking on poor innocent buyers, let's chat a little about the case of the wiley ol' farmer ...

Techno-Geek Rancher

(Adapted from: Smith v. Rickard, 205 Cal.App.3d 1354)

Here we have a software engineer who, unfortunately, didn't work for Google or Twitter or Facebook. So this poor guy didn't have millions and millions of dollars but just enough money that he decided that he wanted to get out of the rat race; that he wanted to get out of the Bay Area. What he really wanted was to move to where things were a little calmer, a little slower.

Our engineer started looking at farm property up around Healdsburg and eventually found a place that had 30 acres—a nice little house, 13 acres of lemon trees, and 15 acres of avocado trees. This was going to be perfect. And the fact that it had income from the orchards to help pay for the mortgage of the house was a good thing because, after all, he didn't get an IPO boost and didn't have gazillions of dollars.

The engineer struck a deal and during the inspections, walked the fields and orchards. He did this with the owner and the real estate broker. He kind of kicked a dirt clod over here and another one over there because after all, he really was a city slicker and not a real farmer.

Even to our engineer, a couple of the trees looked sickly; they looked droopy. They just didn't look—healthy. And he asked the owner if there were any problems with the trees. Old Farmer John, in his beat-up denim dungarees said, "Nah, they're just a little waterlogged. They were over-irrigated, and then there was a rainstorm a little bit ago. So the trees just need to, you know, dry out a little bit."

The engineer looked over at the real estate broker, and the real estate broker asked the seller if there's any evidence of root rot.

The engineer was thinking—"Root rot? What the heck is that?"

It turns out that the real estate broker also owned an avocado orchard and knew that one of the things that can injure trees was this thing called "root rot."

And the seller replied, "Nah, no, not to my knowledge; nothing like that."

With all the assurance of that statement, our engineer closed escrow; and 30 days later, more trees started looking sickly. The buyer started walking around with his foreman, and it turned out about 250 of the trees suffered from root rot.

Within that same 30 days, the foreman went into the barn and started poking around. There he found a 55-gallon barrel of chemicals, which were designed to treat root rot. It was clear that the barrel had been there for a while. A long while.

Clearly Ol' Farmer John, the seller, knew and didn't bother to disclose it.

Now, when the engineer bought this property, the seller carried back financing. Without 250 trees producing avocados for resale, the engineer couldn't make the payments; and Farmer John foreclosed—took the property back.

The engineer was not just a little unhappy—he was pissed. He sued the broker for failure to disclose the fact that there was root rot and the seller for fraud.

The broker claimed that there was no duty for the agent to inspect this property or to do an investigation with respect to the orchard because it was a "commercial property" and the agent's duty of inspection only applied to a "residential property."

The engineer said, "Well, wait just a minute. There's a house right there and that house required the agent to conduct a 'diligent visual inspection;' and if the agent had walked in the barn, the agent would have seen the barrel of chemicals."

"So," the engineer concluded, "the agent breached duty by failing to investigate."

"Plus," he added, "when I asked the agent about the trees, the agent said, 'Well, no root rot.'"

"Did the agent have an obligation to investigate?"—that was the question that the Court of Appeal had to answer.

And the answer was "No, at least not as to the orchard."

First, with regard to the residential property, the court found the agent's duty was limited to the residential portion. The court ruled there was no duty to inspect the barn or orchard because those were commercial properties. And, with regard to the commercial property, the code section that the engineer sued under was to Civil Code section 2079—which only applied to residential duties of inspection and disclosure.

Let's be clear. The engineer's suit was NOT a suit based on breach of fiduciary duty. The court found that because there wasn't a breach of fiduciary duty claim but only a claim based on the violation of the duty to do a diligent inspection of residential property, that the broker had no liability.

The seller, of course, paid through the nose for the fraud.

What's the takeaway here?

The buyer made a mistake in the way that the buyer presented the lawsuit. If the buyer had sued the agent for a common law breach of fiduciary duty, I believe the buyer would have won. I believe that the buyer could have imposed liability on the broker for breaching the fiduciary duty of investigation as a buyer's representative; but because the lawsuit was presented only as a violation of the *listing agent's duty* under Civil Code 2079, the real estate agent got away with no liability.

The counter side to this is that if the real estate agent had the duty to investigate, the real estate agent may have met that duty by asking the seller if there was any root rot. When the seller said "No," that might have met the agent's duty of investigation. But, we'll never know because the Court of Appeal never addressed that question.

What is to be learned from this one?

First, get a good lawyer. If the lawyer had pitched this claim differently, the engineer might have won against the broker.

Second, with respect to commercial property, it is important to know that the agent's duty of disclosure, arising from an investigation due pursuant to section 2079 is limited only to single family houses or a 1 to 4-unit property and does *not* extend beyond that.

So—commercial property brokers get something of a pass with regard to conducting a statutory diligent visual inspection.

8 | Like a Good Neighbor?

From walnut trees in an orchard, we move straight on to other trees -- like the one in your urban neighborhood. You know, the big, leafy one that your neighbor has planted - simply to block your view. Which is just one of the many kinds of things that "good neighbors" can do to torment each other. Think I'm joking? (Nah, you know better by now ...) The next series of cases relate to 'the neighbors from hell' and how the fact that if 'one of those people' lives next door to the house of your dreams, it must be disclosed. No matter how low the price of that dream house will drop as a result.

A Tree Grows in Brooklyn (And Blocks My View, Dammit!)

(Adapted from: Booska v. Patel, 24 Cal.App.4th 1786)

Trees. Everybody likes them. They're big. They're majestic looking. They provide shade in the hot summer. Well, they drop leaves in the fall, and yes, you've got to rake them up; but still, everybody likes trees. Right?

Not everybody.

In fact, there was a guy whose neighbor had a tree—gigantic thing that dropped a lot of leaves. A lot. The roots started to ever so slightly crack some of the concrete walkways in the guy's backyard. So he had a contractor come in, who took an axe and wildly chopped away at 3 feet of the tree's roots along the property line. After all, the roots crossed over onto the guy's property, and he could do whatever he wanted to on his property!

And, you know, there was actually a case out there about trees and about roots that said pretty much that—that an owner had an "absolute right" to remove roots, branches, etc., that were on his land.

Now, as you can imagine, when you chop the roots off of a tree, it will hurt the tree; and this was exactly what happened too. The tree died and had to be removed. And the tree-owner neighbor had to pay for having the tree removed. That tree-owner just happened to be a lawyer (you see where this is going, right?). He sued the pants off the guy that chopped at the roots.

I don't know if he was a good lawyer or not, but at a summary judgment motion, *he lost.* The trial court ruled that the guy who chopped the roots won the case because, the court said, "Here's an old case that says 'absolute right.'"

Sure as darkness follows sunset, the lawyer tree-owner appealed.

And the Court of Appeal announced, "You know, we understand that the rule in law is that you own the property line and everything in the sky above it and everything in the ground below it. We absolutely agree. But there's this other doctrine in law that says, 'You can't exercise your legal right in such a way that will interfere with the legal rights of someone else.' And isn't that what just happened when you axed the neighbor's tree roots and killed his tree?"

There've been a lot of cases, as you might expect, about trees and roots and overhangs and branches falling and all that good stuff.

By and large, the rule has been: If someone else's tree is growing onto your property, you are indeed free to take steps to fix it—to take the branches down or to cut the roots out—but you have to be "reasonable" in the way that you do it.

So in this case, the lawyer won his claim against the neighbor that chopped up his tree, for damages for the loss of the value of the tree itself and for the aesthetic view value that was decreased in the property; and he grew a new tree in that place where the old tree was.

Trees aren't the only kinds of problems folks have encountered with neighbors. Not by a long shot.

Gnarly Neighbors

(Adapted from: Alexander v McKnight,
7 Cal.App.4th 973)

Here is a case where, after a long search, Steven finally found that beautiful house on the end of a cul-de-sac in a bucolic subdivision. The birds were chirping in the trees, the wind was gently blowing through his thinning hair, and you know, it was just gorgeous! He bought it up and was happy as hell—right up until about a week later when he heard this tree-chipping noise, this screech and grind that went on all day long, followed by a neighborhood basketball game that went until the wee hours of the night, and of course, the loud music with the barbecue. And it was repeated … day after day …

And then … Steve started to sniff, on hot summer days, a tar pit smell.

It turned out that Steve's lovely next-door neighbors owned a tree trimming business, and they ran it out of their house. They'd been chipping the logs and the cut trees in their backyard ... for years. And they liked to play basketball, at night, to relax after a hard day's work.

Then they started a dead-car collection that littered the driveway and their front yard.

They also had this deck where they really liked to barbecue, and of course, they'd built that deck without permits. All of which was a violation of the CC&Rs.

But the tar pit smell—that was the thing that took Steve over the edge. He started looking for the source.

Well, it turned out that the neighbors' machines used oil, a fair amount of it, in fact. And the neighbors, well, they didn't want to pay the price of clean disposal of the oil, so they poured it on the roof and hoped that it would just evaporate away.

The nice couple that sold the house to Steve, well, knew about this stuff, but on that transfer disclosure statement, where it asked, "Are you aware of any neighborhood noise or problems or nuisances?"—the seller marked "No."

Really?

The Court of Appeal described these folks as "overtly hostile neighbors who enjoyed tormenting the neighborhood." It noted that it had been going on for years. The question was:

Did the real estate broker, did the agent, did the seller—did anybody—have an obligation to disclose the fact of the crappy neighbors?

Now think about it. The listing agent had an obligation to try to maximize the price that the seller could get for the real estate. If she disclosed the nasty neighbors, the value was going to go down the toilet. If she, well, didn't disclose the nasty neighbors, the value might match the rest of the stuff in the neighborhood. What was she supposed to do?

She was supposed to disclose.

The Court of Appeal talked about valuation of a property—the intrinsic value of a property—like where you can say, "George Washington slept here." That increases the value, the court noted. It's subjective, certainly. Similarly, it noted that nasty neighbors decrease the value of a property. It's subjective too, but both are material facts that have to be disclosed if they exist.

The interesting thing about this case was the court granted damages—the decrease in value of the real estate—because of the neighbors. The court also issued an injunction requiring the bad neighbors to behave themselves. And the bad neighbors appealed!

They asked, "How come it is that you're going to subject us to paying damages for a decrease in value, but once of course we comply with the 'we must behave order,' there's no longer a decrease in value? So the seller is going to get a windfall—

we're going to have to behave, and they're going to get $24,000 of our money."

And the Court of Appeal agreed with them! The court decided, "You're right, it's a double recovery; and you can't have that."

"But you know," the court went on to say, "the trial court never ruled on the amount of damages for the emotional distress that you caused Steve," and sent the case back to the trial court for further review on the amount of damages for emotional distress.

One can only imagine if the emotional distress damages were more than the decrease in value damages. Far more.

So what is to be learned from this one?

We learn that sometimes no good deed goes unpunished. The brokerage/agent is responsible for disclosing all the known facts affecting value or desirability, even (or, perhaps, especially) the ones that they would really prefer not to because they know it's going to make a sale more difficult.

"Call the Cops!"

(Adapted from: Shapiro v. Sutherland,
64 Cal.App.4th 1534)

You know how IBM had that banner—their tagline was "THINK." Here's a story about an IBM guy that maybe needed to think twice about what he tried to do.

IBM had an arrangement with a national real estate company that if it needed to relocate one of its executives, the real estate company would try to sell the house. If it didn't sell quickly, the real estate company would in turn buy the house from the executive (based on the appraised value of the house) and then sell it off later. That's exactly what happened in this case. The IBM executive got transferred out of the state, couldn't sell the house, three appraisals were made and the value was determined, and the real estate company bought it. Several months later, the property was re-sold—at a loss by the way. The real estate company couldn't get it sold for the same value of the appraisals and lost $99,000 on the deal.

To add insult to injury, shortly after the deal closed, the buyer discovered some things that the seller had failed to mention. Like the neighbors—who, well, weren't the nicest neighbors to have. They regularly had really loud, booze-fueled, late night barbecues, coupled with the late night arguments—that went on and on and on.

Turned out, this wasn't something new. In fact, it was discovered that the IBM executive had called the cops on the neighbors dozens of times before he sold the house.

But, you know, on that part of the transfer disclosure statement that asked: "Are you aware of any neighborhood conditions or nuisances?" he said, "No." I guess I would have too, if I wanted to hide it from everybody.

So what happened to the buyers? Frankly, they just didn't want to live there at all after about a week. They sued the IBM guy and sued the real estate company, which was actually "the seller" of the property to them.

Both of those defendants filed what's called a "demur," a motion with the court that basically said, "Dismiss the case because we have no potential liability."

The real estate company argued, "We never made any disclosures. We never had an obligation to make any disclosures about the neighborhood because, well, we've never lived there."

The seller said, "I didn't sell to these people; I sold to the real estate company. So I never made any representations to the second buyer; therefore, how could I possibly have made any misrepresentation to them?"

The trial court agreed with both of those defenses and kicked the case out.

So the buyers appealed. The Court of Appeal looked at things a little bit differently.

The Court of Appeal said that the IBM executive knew that the real estate company was merely a transitional owner of the home and that it was going to turn over whatever seller disclosure documents it got from the IBM executive to whoever the ultimate buyer would be. The appellate court further said that the trial court misconstrued evidence with respect to what was meant when the seller signed the transfer document. The appellate court noted that when the seller signed the deed, he didn't name the real estate company as the buyer; he left it blank, knowing that whoever was going to be the ultimate buyer would have their name filled in on the grant deed. That evidenced, the court argued, the seller's intention and recognition of the fact that the property wasn't being "sold" to the real estate company but rather to the second buyer from the real estate company.

Did the real estate company get out of liability on this case completely? Nope. In fact, it had to stay in the lawsuit—not because it had liability for nondisclosure but because the buyer was suing for rescission—which means "undoing the deal." It was possible that the real estate company was going to get the property back, so that they could re-sell it, again, to yet someone else. (But this time, with adequate disclosures.)

How does a brokerage protect itself from lying clients? It's hard. Are there other situations where the brokerage can find itself in between a rock and a hard spot? Sure. Imagine the following scenario:

The brokerage had an agent that did an inspection of property as part of a bank foreclosure, back when the only way an agent (and a brokerage!) could make a living was by giving a "broker's opinion of value" to banks—hoping to get the listing from the bank when it was time to sell that property off.

As part of that broker's opinion of value, it was noted that there was a leaking roof and a crack in the foundation. When the broker handed that document to the bank, the bank said, "Thank you very much," and it tucked it away in the file.

The agent hadn't sold anything for three years, got out of the business, and was last seen selling paint at OSH. The current designated broker for the corporate brokerage was put in the job just a year earlier.

The bank, eventually, got around to listing the property with the brokerage. The broker in charge had no idea about the former agent's report. Somebody else in the company got the listing and sold the property.

The buyer, after it finally rained in California, learned of the faulty roof because of massive leaks, then sued both the bank and the brokerage for damages because of the faulty roof and the cracked foundation, and said, pointing at the broker's opinion of value it obtained from the bank through discovery, that the bank knew about it and hadn't disclosed it. The buyer claimed that the brokerage knew about it too and didn't disclose it.

The bank was screwed because right there, in its file, was the report.

But what about the brokerage? Did the brokerage "know"? Did the brokerage anticipate that the report "it" provided to the bank, years ago, would be used or discoverable? Should the report have been disclosed to a subsequent buyer as a "material fact" disclosure?

I think the answer is "Yup."

If the brokerage had information related to a transaction that was done years ago, or an inspection that was done years ago, the brokerage had an obligation to disclose that to any subsequent client, including the after-foreclosure purchaser.

Think about that, and it might just keep you awake till 3:00 in the morning.

How many reports, how many files, are in a large corporate brokerage? Does a brokerage have an obligation to disclose a termite report done for a property it sold last year? Five years ago? Ten years ago?

If the reports show that there is a continuing problem in a certain area of the house, is that a "red flag" that might indicate a poor design that traps water and leads to rot? Would releasing the reports and revealing this "history" of repeated problems be "material"?

How many brokerages have a system of tracking the addresses of former sales? And what about files on properties that had inspections but never closed? Are those reports to be delivered to a subsequent client?

There are no clear answers to some of those questions.

9 | To Be or Not To Be (the Designated Broker)

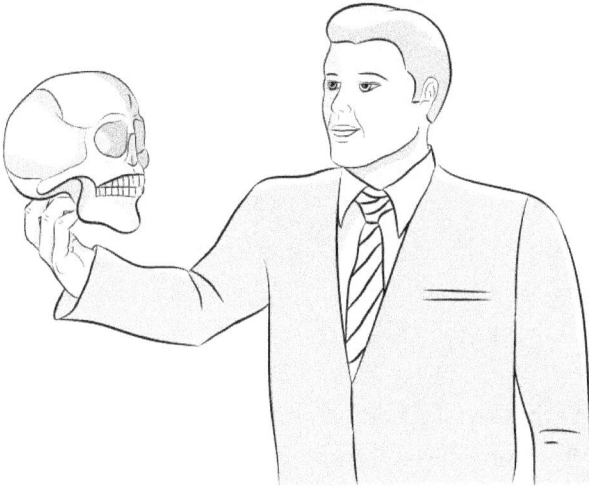

To be large and in charge! The master of your own destiny! The Boss! To get a percentage (even a small one) of the work and earnings of hundreds of agents. How cool is that? Very ... for some.

For others, managing a real estate brokerage, being the designated broker—the one that the CalBRE picks on if there is a regulatory issue—can be like herding cats that are on fire while being chased by a pack of hungry wolves.

The California Department of Consumer Affairs is the overseer of the Bureau of Real Estate. Think about that. And be afraid. (As Hamlet was, when speaking of Yorick.)

When a customer is unhappy, who are they gonna call? "Who's in charge over there?"—that's who. And when that customer files suit, even if the designated broker had nothing to do with the transaction … well, who cares about details like that … the designated broker gets named too.

Panic? Not yet. Not … yet.

Here are a couple of cases that are or should be near and dear to every broker's heart, especially if you are the designated broker of a corporate brokerage.

Remember that while companies can be licensed by the California Bureau of Real Estate, there has to be a flesh and blood person that is responsible to the CalBRE for anything that the corporate real estate brokerage does. Well, that makes sense, right? After all, the State needs to be able to pick on somebody or get somebody on the phone.

Here are two different cases where the designated broker was sued on behalf of a customer of the brokerage.

Personal Liability: Here, You Take It

(Adapted from: Meyer v. Holley, 537 US 280)

In the first of these cases, an interracial couple was attempting to purchase a home. The agent within the brokerage refused to serve them; she simply refused to present their proposals for the purchase of the house. They sued under the federal Fair Housing Act.

They sued the designated broker as well because under the federal Fair Housing Act, the law says that anyone who has "control over the entity" that is engaging in the discrimination has liability; and the couple identified the person the (then) Department of Real Estate Regulations in California as the "designated broker" (the person responsible for oversight and supervision of all the agents within the brokerage) as the person "in control."

The designated broker had nothing to do with the deal that the agent was involved with when the discriminatory act was undertaken. In fact, there wasn't any evidence that the couple had ever met the designated broker, yet the federal court found the designated broker liable.

Well, he appealed, and the Ninth Circuit Court of Appeal agreed with the trial court. And so the designated broker appealed again, and surprise of all surprises, the United States Supreme Court took that case. It held that the designated broker was *not* responsible, even though the federal Fair Housing Act said anyone who had "control" over someone who was discriminating would also have liability because of a public policy to broaden the scope of those who could have liability.

The Supreme Court said that mere designation by a regulatory agency as the person in control wasn't sufficient.

So the case was sent back to the district court—the federal district court—to see if there was any other kind of relationship between the designated broker and the agent that could possibly give rise to "control" *other than* the mere regulatory oversight requirement.

And the district court found that there *was* additional evidence of control and found the real estate broker responsible.

What was that control?

It turned out that the designated broker was really a "rent-a-broker" for all intents and purposes. He had owned the brokerage, but he was selling the brokerage—to the very agent that was doing the discriminatory practices. The former owner-broker had pretty much abandoned the brokerage. He had delegated all of the oversight responsibilities to this agent, who then discriminated.

The district court said that under "principal and agency law," which is different than the real estate agency law, because the designated broker delegated the oversight responsibility to the agent, the designated broker could be held responsible for the improper action of the agent. The theory was that the agent had been designated the "agent" of the "broker" for all oversight purposes, not "just" regulatory obligations.

That got every designated broker in California nervous. Really nervous.

Personal Liability: Umm, No Thanks.

(Adapted from: Sandler v. Sanchez,
206 Cal.App.4th 1431)

Fast forward a couple of years—in another case, this time in the California state system, there was an agent of a corporate brokerage who was working with a couple to help them loan money. The agent arranged a loan from that couple to someone else doing a rehab of a piece of property.

The agent told the lender-client that the $600,000 that was being lent would be enough to do the rehab work and that the property was going to be immediately re-sold. Everybody would be repaid; it would all be good.

It turned out that the $600,000 was not nearly enough to complete the rehab.

One of the reasons it wasn't enough was that the agent took $300,000 of it and embezzled it. (I guess that would hurt any kind of budget.)

The couple that had lent the $600,000 was unhappy. They knew that the agent was broke, so they sued the designated broker, using this earlier federal court case as kind of a bootstrap argument as to why the designated broker would have responsibility.

They made the same claim—that because the CalBRE regulations required the designated broker to oversee the agents within the brokerage, that designated broker had responsibility to them—personal responsibility to them—for the losses that they suffered as a result of the agent's bad act.

It is important to note that an innocent corporation *has* liability for the fraudulent acts of its agents/employees if those acts were done while the agent/employee was apparently acting on behalf of the corporation.

Here, however, the customer was suing the designated broker, personally, NOT on behalf of the corporate brokerage.

To the claims made by the lender-customer, the California Court of Appeal said, "No."

"While we appreciate the federal court's opinion with regard to whether or not a designated broker of a corporate brokerage would have responsibility for the act of an agent," it said, "that's not the way we interpret California law." It found that the broker had no personal liability to the customer of the brokerage.

With regard to the federal case, the California Court of Appeal explained, "While that's federal law and while the Fair Housing Act may have a broader definition of "control" because it—the federal government—wants to impose, as a matter of public policy, stricter liability for enforcement of the Fair Housing Act, this wasn't a federal question case and it wasn't a question under the Fair Housing Act. This process was about making the loans." Thus the corporate broker had no responsibility.

This is a case that provides tremendous shelter for the personal liability of a designated broker of a corporate brokerage. And that's one of the reasons why perhaps having a corporation as the brokerage isn't such a bad idea.

Lest you think that being a designated broker is a "fun" gig, filled with power lunches and runs to the bank to deposit all the commissions from all your worker-bee agents, it is important to know that the broker is responsible for all kinds of other issues too. It is not always ... "Fun."

A Dead End Job?

(Adapted from: A True Story)

This story came, not from some stodgy legal case, but, rather, from the general counsel of a San Francisco brokerage house. He relayed the events at one of our *War Story Wednesdays* seminars.

The broker of the corporate brokerage was sitting at her desk one afternoon when she got a call from an experienced agent. The agent wanted to know if the sidewalk in front of a house actually counted as part of the "house"—for that rule that said you had to disclose a death "in the house."

With her curiosity piqued, the broker had the agent come into the office and explain why he was asking the question.

It turned out that two guys, partners, living in San Francisco, were selling their 4 million-dollar house and had an accepted offer, and even a backup offer. But they were unhappy. With each other. They were having a fight while leaving the house on the way to the gym, and they got into the car and pulled out of the garage.

Then one said to the other that he had forgotten his gym bag in the house, so he left the car to go into the house to get it. But when he returned to the car, it was via the third story window he jumped out of. Splat. Onto the sidewalk. Dead.

Hence the agent's question of the broker: Is that a death "in the house" that *has to be* disclosed?

Holy smokes. The broker figured the pending deal was dead. (Pardon the pun.) She was certain of the need to explain to the buyers (devout Buddhists) and the backup offerors of the death. She anticipated a reduced listing price, by half a million, and having to deal with a probate Executor too. Great. Just great.

So the broker started making calls. The sister/cousin/aunt (I don't remember) of the decedent lived in Florida and said that she would come right out. She was shocked and unhappy. It was a lot to deal with, she explained.

The Buddhist buyers gave the broker a second shock—they still wanted the house! But they also wanted their monk to come out and cleanse the unhappy spirit. So they arranged a meeting. The monk came with bells and incense and performed the equivalent of an exorcism. The buyers now felt even more "in tune" with the property. They wanted to continue with the purchase. All was good. Whew.

But the decedent's sister/cousin/aunt, whatever, was a different situation. She ended up living in the house while clearing up the estate, and it was wearing on her. She was unhappy, confused, and out of her depth. She made more and more demands on the broker and agent. Those demands became more random as time passed. Finally, she called and told them to come to the house, that she was ready to sign the damn papers and just end the process.

So off they went, the agent and his assistant.

Ding-Dong. The doorbell got no answer. They used the lockbox key and went on in.

"Hello?"

No answer.

The agent went to the back of the house; the assistant, upstairs. And then the scream from the assistant—the sister/cousin/aunt had hung herself!

I kid you not. You can't make this stuff up.

The broker was, once again, sure that this deal was a goner. Sure as daylight, the buyers cried, "Enough!" and backed out. Would you blame them?

A million. The broker was sure the house had just lost a million dollars in value. There was one more call to make—to the backup offerors who said ... they wanted the house anyway. No reduction in sales price. No Buddhist monk. Maybe just a little paint and carpeting. A happy ending after all.

I was telling this story one night at my yacht club, and a longtime broker in San Francisco was nodding her head all along. Then she told me, "You forgot one part."

"Oh?"

"Yeah. The house was on a cul-de-sac. The second buyers asked the City to remove the sign that said 'Dead End.'"

The City did.

10 | Buyer Beware?

Let's talk about an "as is" sale.

Now, back in the olden days, you could sell a property "as is," and it really meant "Buyer beware." You were telling a buyer, "You're buying a pig in a poke—if you could find a poke and if you had a pig."

Well, things have changed—a lot—in California.

Back in the olden days, you could have a one-page purchase contract (email me and I'll show you one from the 1970s), and a real estate broker could simply say, "Agent suggests buyer gets all inspections necessary to completely satisfy the buyer with respect to the condition of the property"—and that was it.

Not so much anymore.

Nowadays, there are all kinds of statutory provisions that require, among other things, a transfer disclosure statement. A TDS has got a lot of questions in it, which the seller is required to respond to (truthfully), thus advising the buyer about the condition of the property. The seller is to describe its characteristics—really, to describe its flaws.

But if you want to sell a property "as is" without going through the drill of having inspections made or to fill out the form, can you?

"As Is" My A$$

(Adapted from: Loughrin v. Barr, 15 Cal.App.4th 1188)

In one case not so long ago, a seller tried to do just that—create an "as is" purchase and include language in that purchase agreement that said that neither the seller nor the seller's broker were making *any* representations, express or implied, about the condition of the property. If the buyer wanted to learn about the property, the form said, the buyer would have to conduct its own inspections, at its own cost, and could not rely on anything said by or received from the seller or the broker.

The buyer, of course, bought the property. And, don't you know it—found problems in the slab, in the foundation, and in the flooring—and sued. (Shock and dismay!)

The trial court looked at the purchase agreement, looked at the "as is" provision, looked at the waiver of any claims' language that was in it, and decided, "Too bad, Mr. Buyer, you agreed that you were buying this property 'as is,' so you had the duty to do those investigations. You assumed the risk that there would be something that was undisclosed."

Our litigious society being what it is, the buyer appealed. The Court of Appeal looked at the scenario differently.

The Court of Appeal first addressed the issue of whether or not the transfer disclosure statutes, 2079 and 1102 in the civil code, could be waived at all. Some statutory provisions that give protections to "a class of the public" cannot be waived, as a matter of public policy. Whether the statutory transfer disclosure requirements were one of that "class" of protections hadn't been considered before.

It turns out, the court decided, that the real estate purchase agreement and the transfer disclosure language in the statute were *not* deemed a public purpose, so the requirements could, indeed, be waived. "Okay," breathed the seller.

The court went on, "So if you can waive the obligation to provide a TDS and waive the obligation to make those statutory disclosures, what's the language in the waiver that you have to use?"

Here, the court noted, the language was fairly broad, right? The buyer "waived all representations, express or implied, about the condition of the property."

Then the Court of Appeal said, "You know, to have a waiver, it has to be a knowing, voluntary, and intelligent one." "Knowing" means that you have to describe *all of the claims that are being waived*, and, in this case, wouldn't that include claims regarded as negligent misrepresentations or be limited to just unknown factors in the real estate?"

After all, it is against public policy to waive intentional misrepresentations. You can't lie, knowing that you're lying, and have a provision in an agreement that says you can't be sued for having lied.

You can make a mistake, you can be *negligent* in what you represent, and you can create a waiver of liability for your *negligence,* but you have to be very express *in that waiver* and must state that the claims that are being waived include negligence and negligent misrepresentation claims.

The court looked at the waiver and decided, "This waiver didn't do that," so the seller was found responsible for the damages.

In terms of real estate transactions, it has been my experience that the courts look to the substance of the representations that are being made. Even if there was an "as is" provision, and even if there was waiver language, like in this case, I think that a seller or a real estate broker would be incredibly hard-pressed to take protection behind a waiver from a buyer—even if the waiver expressly referred to "negligence" and "negligent misrepresentations."

Don't rely on a waiver—that's the short answer.

11 | The End (of the Beginning)

And so we wrap up this edition of War Story Wednesdays.

I covered a lot of material in this first volume. I can almost guarantee there will be another, and probably another after that. In fact, as we went to press, there was yet another case of a brokerage that got nailed where one agent who was representing a seller, and another who was representing a buyer, and the court deemed the *listing* agent a "fiduciary" of the buyer! Holy smokes. I can hardly wait to get into the details of that one.

The fun part about this project (if writing a book can *ever* be considered fun, just ask my editor) was talking with various brokers and clients about the cases and hearing their stories. Volume 2 will, if all goes as planned, be a collection of "real life" stories like "A Dead End Job?" If you've got one, let me know. Who knows, yours might make it to print in the next edition.

In the meantime, as Sergeant Esterhaus would say: "Be careful out there."

About the Author

Who am I? Why do I do this? What does someone get when my staff and I are hired? Am I any good at this lawyer stuff? Will I win? Those are all good questions—and I even have answers for some of them.

I started my firm in the mid-1990s after the Savings and Loan implosion killed commercial real estate for about five years. Before that, I'd been selling commercial and residential real estate.

In 1978, I got my California real estate license and two years later, my broker's license. In 1993, I was awarded the nationally recognized CCIM designation by the Commercial Investment Real Estate Institute. In 1997, I was admitted to practice law in California and founded Hanson Law Firm.

I started the Firm to represent and defend real estate brokers, and it still does. I'll also sue the pants off of them when it is appropriate to do so. I truly believe that the real estate professional ought to be professional and that a customer is entitled to rely on that presumed professionalism. If a broker or agent doesn't live up to that standard and, as a result, damages a customer, then, well, they ought to be spanked.

Defending and suing brokers, and taking on cases they referred to us from their customers was and is a big part of my business. But as the market changed drastically, so did the Firm's, and my, focus. When insurance carriers began making wholesale denials of claims made by my brokerage clients, I started suing the very carriers who were supposed to protect those brokerages. Successfully. Recent examples include a recovery of $1,000,000 for one brokerage client from a TOPA Insurance bad faith claim and a second $625,000 settlement from Lloyds of London on behalf of a client of a brokerage. As defense counsel, I've had plaintiffs' attorneys sanctioned over $13,000 for filing frivolous lawsuits against my broker clients.

I'm an experienced trial lawyer, not just a litigator. I'm not afraid of (and actually enjoy) being in a courtroom. I've been called ingenious, tenacious, and strategic. I'll take those accolades. The other side calls me a mean pain in the ass who acts like a junk-yard dog and creates "issues" just to cause them trouble. I really feel bad about that.

To give you a sense of who I am, I'll share these few insights and experiences. At 6, I taught myself how to ride a bicycle by propping it up against the wall of the house and riding like hell down the driveway—praying I could make the corner onto the sidewalk and not go flying into the street. At 16, I learned how to SCUBA dive without knowing how to swim. At 32, I rode a motorcycle across the country for ten months, without ever having ridden before. At 34, I enrolled in a nighttime law school, and, while working fulltime, was still the editor-in-chief of the school's law review, all with only one year of undergraduate credits to my name. Three years later, I started this law practice, which has grown to include additional attorneys, statewide, and has thrived for 15+ years. At 48, I decided sailboat racing was my next interest, so I crewed on several ocean races down the California coast. Because I remain a confirmed power boater, I recently applied for and received my USCG 100 Ton Master's License. (No, I'm not changing careers again, to drive the Golden Gate Ferry.) The point is—I simply don't believe in the phrase: "You can't do that."

I've won cases I should have lost and lost cases I should have won. I don't give up. I don't often give in. What I believe, more than anything else, is that if you've been wronged, you should be allowed to recover. If you hire me and my staff, you get our best effort. While that may not always be enough, it's a lot. I'm happy to say that most of our clients have walked away from the gut-wrenching experience of a lawsuit knowing and feeling that we've done our very best for them.

I'm often asked, "Who have you done work for?"

Here is a representative list of clients:

- RE/MAX Gold
- Century 21- Landmark
- Exit Realty – Carson
- Mason Management
- Centers Dynamic
- Alameda Realty
- Juvon Realty

- Homes and Land 4 U
- 4 Rivers Realty
- California Loan Associates
- Golden Key Funding
- Home Funders
- Infinity Realty
- ARR, Inc
- New Vision Realty
- United One Mortgage
- West Management
- Boston Market
- American Radio Systems
- Favorite Brands Foods
- Connecticut General Life Insurance Company
- AETNA Life Insurance Company
- DHL, Corp.
- Wells Fargo Bank
- Bank One Arizona
- American Dehydrated Onion & Garlic Association
- GCE Commercial, Inc.
- Catalyst Group, LLC
- Gold Coast Interiors, Inc.

Here is a partial and representative selection of clients I represented in my capacity as a commercial real estate broker:

- Kaiser Permanente
- Doric Development
- Banner Development
- Avery-Dennison

- Shidler Group

Following in Appendix A, more importantly for someone looking for a trial lawyer, is a list of most of my trial results.

Appendix A: Trial Win/Loss Record

W	L	Opposing Counsel	Nature of Case
	L	Bernard, Balgley, etc	Leibowitz - Rheinheimer (Trial) 7 Consolidated cases alleging "alter ego" liability against former owners of non-judicial trustee corporation
?	?	Bernard, Balgley, etc	Leibowitz - Rheinheimer (On Appeal)
W		Allen, Matkins, etc	PAA - Santiago In breach of fiduciary duty claim, and related indemnity claim against agents by brokerage, obtained favorable settlement and indemnity judgment.
W		Steyer, Lowenthal, etc	Kahan - Zollars (Trial) Successfully obtained unlawful detainer judgment against former owner of foreclosed property who claimed Bank errors in re-sale of property.

W	L	Opposing Counsel	Nature of Case
W		McCarthy & Holthus	Kahan - US Bank (Quiet Title) Bank foreclosed on second position deed of trust; re-sold the REO property; then foreclosed on pre-existing, and undisclosed, first position deed of trust. Obtained judgment in favor of third party bidder at second sale.
W		Boutin Jones, LLP and Boss Law Firm	Kahan - US Bank (Appeal) Successfully defended underlying judgment in favor of bidder against Bank assertion that 'professional bidder' could never be deemed a bonafide purchaser in non-judicial foreclosure sale.
	L	McCormick, Barstow	Cassady - C21 Claim of breach of fiduciary duty when real estate broker allowed ex-husband of client to invade commercial property and steal all the equipment and inventory of family business.

W	L	Opposing Counsel	Nature of Case
	L	Ginder, Sunderland, etc	Hermann - Lynch Claim of prescriptive easement of 'logging trail' notwithstanding access and title to deeded, but unimproved, adjacent roadway easement.
W		Alborg & Dictor	Belli - Mason MacDuffie (Trial) Successfully defended claimed breach of fiduciary duty for alleged failure to present purchase offer.
W		Alborg & Dictor	Belli - Mason MacDuffie (Appeal) Successfully defended underlying judgment against finding of breach of fiduciary duty claim.
W		Babbit & Walter	Howell - Oakland Properties Obtained breach of contract and fraud judgment (with punitive damages) against attorneys/brokers in claims related to real property redevelopment.

W	L	Opposing Counsel	Nature of Case
	L*	L.O. of L. Horton	Waugh - Ingersol Rand Successfully defended against a $6,000,000 claim for damages where only $6,000 was awarded plaintiff.
W		Bailey & Brown	Woolmington Smith - Erickson Realty † Successfully resolved, after commencement of trial, dispute related to breach of contract and fraud on real property easement and subdividability claims.
W		L. Finley	Cote - (Injunction) Prevailed in obtaining civil restraining orders against nut-case plaintiffs who fire bombed our offices, and threatened to kill client.
W		L. Finley	Cote - Finley (Injunction - Appeal) Prevailed in appeal of issuance of restraining orders.
W		L. Finley	Cote - Finley (Defamation) Prevailed in defense of defamation claims brought by defendants.

W	L	Opposing Counsel	Nature of Case
W		L.O. of L. Nelson	Cote - Realty World (Broker) Prevailed in obtaining judgment against real estate brokerage for breach of fiduciary duty and fraud in case involving six separate properties.
W		Robins, Kaplan, etc	Cote - Lloyds of London (Insurance) ‡ Obtained $650,000 settlement before trial from Lloyds of London, et al, third party, refusal to defend, 'bad faith' claim.
W		Selman - Breitman	RE/Max - TOPA ‡ Obtained $1,000,000 settlement before trial from TOPA Insurance et al, in first-party, refusal to defend, 'bad faith' claim.
W		Miller Law Firm	Fields - RE/Max ‡ Obtained dismissal after $13,000 sanction awarded against plaintiffs counsel for filing frivolous claims.
W		Miller Law Firm	Langdon - RE/Max ‡ Obtained dismissal after $13,000 sanction awarded against plaintiffs counsel for filing frivolous claims.

W	L	Opposing Counsel	Nature of Case
W		Johnson / Christensen	Lair - Hendrickson † Obtained dismissal at opening statements in breach of fiduciary claim against real estate broker.
	L	Johnson / Christensen	Hendrickson (Appeal) Claim for contractual and statutory attorney fees in regard to dismissed breach of fiduciary duty claim of former clients against real estate broker.
W		L.O. of J. Roveda	Beasley - Bell Successfully obtained judgment against partner/developer in Oakland redevelopment project.
W		John Younger	HLF - Accolo Successfully obtained breach of contract award in binding arbitration.
W		Records Destroyed	Moyer Realty - Choy Successfully obtained possession of commercial property from tenant who had earlier developed successful "Ponzi scheme" of revolving tenancies as a vehicle to retain possession without rent payment, for years.

W	L	Opposing Counsel	Nature of Case
	L	Latham, Watkins, etc	**Thaler - Hidalgo (Trial)** Claim by a professional investor who attempted to voluntarily pay reinstatement amounts on property in foreclosure in order to create opportunity to purchase.
	L	Latham, Watkins, etc	**Thaler - Hidalgo (Appeal)** Claim by a professional investor who attempted to voluntarily pay reinstatement amounts on property in foreclosure in order to create opportunity to purchase.
W		L.O. of R. Rommell	**Wolf - Marsh** Successful eviction of recalcitrant tenant.
W		L.O. of R. Kahn	**Commodore - EDD** Successfully defended claim by State that additional taxes were due to it as a result of employer's use of independent contractors.
W		State of CA	**Commodore - BCDC** Successfully defended claim that utility barges constituted "bay fill."

W	L	Opposing Counsel	Nature of Case
W		Ryan & Lifter	Holcomb - Jackson Successfully defended claim of negligence brought by customer of general contractor.
W		L.O. of J. Aguilar	Billon - Marborough Successfully obtained possession of commercial property.
W		T. Dronkers	Dronkers - Muir Street Successfully defended claim of breach of fiduciary duty.
W		State of CA	Siptrott - DRE Successfully defended against attempted license revocation.
	L	State of CA	McBride - DRE Accusation of breach of regulatory duties.
W		State of CA	Valdez - Labor Board Successfully defended against claimed regulatory violations.
	L	Reed Smith	Carol Williams - Prentiss Prop. Unsuccessful defense against claimed assignment of commercial lease without consent.

W	L	Opposing Counsel	Nature of Case
	L	Reed Smith	Carol Williams - Baker Law Group Unsuccessful defense against claimed assignment of commercial lease without consent.
W		L.O. of J. Latini	Patel v Ashray Successful defense against claim of fraud in inducement to entry of purchase of hotel.
	L	L.O. of M. Normoyle	Johnston - Morelli (Appeal) Claimed failure of formation of purchase agreement.
W		State of CA	Peavich - OAH Successful defense of attempt to revoke professional license.
	L		In Re: Estate of Collins Loss of collateral assignment of inheritance due to estate attorney's malfeasance.

W	L	Opposing Counsel	Nature of Case

(*)   While, technically, a "loss" - defending a $6M claim down to a $6K verdict felt more like a "win" to the client. (Me too.)

(‡)   The "settlements" in these cases obtained the *complete relief* sought by the client, without the need for trial.

(†) These cases settled favorably for the client, after trial commenced, but before verdicts were issued; no cases that settled before trial commenced are included in the list.

Disclaimers

What would a book written by a lawyer be without disclaimers?

I am NOT your lawyer.

Reading this book does NOT make me your lawyer.

You should consider the case stories in this book pure works of fiction. You should NOT rely on the stories in this book as "accurate" (or even inaccurate) representations of the cases, or the law that resulted from the cases.

How'm I doin' so far?

Here's the point. The California State Bar has lots of Rules about when an attorney-client relationship is formed. This book isn't a thing that does that. Sending me an email because you read this book, WILL NOT do that. By the way, if you send me an email because of this book, it WILL NOT be deemed confidential. I will be free to blab about anything you write to me. To anybody. I may even put it in the second (or third) edition of this book. Without asking you for permission to do so first. (BTW, if you have a great story you want to share, do send it on over. I'm always looking for new material... and I just might print it in the next edition!)

The State Bar has Rules about a lawyer's solicitation of work The Rules give me a headache. They are written by lawyers, to regulate lawyers. (Can you possibly imagine what Rules, designed to do that, read like? They are awful. They would give you a headache too.) You should not, and I do not, consider this book a solicitation for your business.

As I said in the Introduction, if you want real legal advice, contact a lawyer, create an attorney-client relationship by way of a written retainer agreement, write a whopping large retainer check, and hire yourself a lawyer. If you want to hire me, we'll talk about it. No guarantees. First, we'll make an appointment, we'll talk about your case at that appointment, and *then* we'll decide about working together. Then; not now.

Whew.

(I hope that will satisfy the State Bar.)

Stay in Touch

The topics covered in this book are also reviewed in a (mostly) monthly electronic newsletter we publish. If you'd like to be on that list, or if you have a "war story" for me, or if you'd like to talk to me about a specific situation, reach out to me through any of the methods below. (And, no, we don't sell the list or make it available to anyone else. Period.) When you sign up, I will also give you access to selected video presentations of these and other *War Stories*, and, occasionally, a presentation we've done at some conference or other. To get updates to this book, to get the newsletter, or to reach me and tell me your personal *War Story*, visit:

·   www.WarStoryWednesdays.com or
·   text WSW to 58885 or
·   text your name and email to (415) 942-8291

www.ingramcontent.com/pod-product-compliance
Lightning Source LLC
Chambersburg PA
CBHW062024200326
41519CB00017B/4923